LOVE CONVERSATIONS:

Christian Perspectives about Love and Relationships

Sylvia L. Daniels

Love Conversations: Christian Perspectives about Love and Relationships

Published by Strategic Diversity, L.L.C.

Copyright © 2018 by Sylvia L. Daniels

For more information about Love Conversations, visit SylviaLDaniels.com or LoveConversations.Love

ISBN: 13 9780692145449

Editors: Wynter S. Thomas and Marycoole

Publisher:
Strategic Diversity, L.L.C.
P.O. Box 47680
Oak Park, MI, 48237

Strategic Diversity LLC

While the author has made every effort to provide accurate telephone number, internet address and mailing address information at the time of publication, neither the publisher nor the author assumes any responsibility for errors or changes that occur after publication. Furthermore, neither the author nor publisher have any control or assume responsibility for third-party Web sites or content.

Some names and identifying characteristics have been changed to protect the privacy of the individuals involved.

PRINTED IN THE UNITED STATES OF AMERICA

ACKNOWLEDGEMENTS

I thought the acknowledgments would be the easiest thing for me to write. But it isn't. Like many before me, remembering everyone that has played a major role in my life is a daunting task. If I've forgotten a name, please remember my intentions. I appreciate you just the same.

To my Abba (my Father God) the one who loves me first, last and the most – You've drawn me to you with loving kindness. You've been there through the good times and comforted me when tears were my only food and drink. You've made me victorious when my enemies looked for my downfall. You spoke your heart and destiny over me and what you've said stands true forever. You will always be there, and because of that, I have enduring love. I can't begin to thank you enough Abba, but thank and praise you I will!

To each of you who anonymously shared your perspectives and your life stories, your inputs are invaluable, and I so appreciate that! Your transparency was a gift to me, and so it is to those who are reading this book now. Thank you for trusting me with your stories, your advice, and your hearts. I've learned a lot from you. It has been a true honor.

To my children – Khalaya, Khiyon, and Khalif Jr. – You are the greatest blessings in my life because being your mom has allowed me to experience unconditional love – both giving and receiving it. I'm so incredibly proud of who you are and I look forward to seeing who you will become. Go Forward!

To my friends – Arlette & Mark Willis, Keisha Dukes, Kwan Dukes-Reese, Rita Fields, Meredith Harper, Samona Perry, Randy Walker, Eric Wheelwright, Jocelyn Giangrande and Anton Chastang – Thank you all for sharing your wisdom, praying for me, challenging me and encouraging me to think deeper and grow stronger. You all have been great examples to me. I love, appreciate and respect each of you very much!

Bishop Elect Marvin L. Winans – Your godly words of wisdom and kindness meant a lot to me in my darkest hours and they resonate still today. Thank you!

To my family – Tahesha Davis, Veronica King, Edward Davis, Toure & Betsy Davis; Sylvia Reynolds-Blakely & Raymond Blakely and James S. Reynolds Sr. – I appreciate the fun times and the love we all share with one another. Let's continue to grow together.

To my love Clarence Ray – Thank you for showing me what love, kindness and respect in a relationship looks and feels like. Your strength, love, care and protection of me mean more than I can say. You are truly a rare breed, and I'm so grateful for the opportunity to know and love you. You are simply amazing!

To my daughter Khalaya Daniels - Thank you for listening and giving me on-the-spot feedback. I appreciate your support during my 1:00 am writing and editing marathons. You are wise beyond your years. You've meant so much to this project and I appreciate it!

Kwaun Dukes-Reese, Anton Lewis, LaShun Franklin, Keisha Dukes, Katie Naeyaert and Arlette Willis - Thank you all for reviewing my manuscript and providing your input. I chose you because I trust your honesty and frankness.

To my friend Eric Wheelwright - I couldn't have ask for a better friend. Your godly wisdom, challenging perspectives and unwavering faith in me have been invaluable. I appreciate all that you've sown into my life. May God return it to you a thousand times over.

Wynter S. Thomas and Marycoole - Thank you very much for the work you did to bring Love Conversations together. I truly appreciate your time and expertise as editors for each phase of this project.

To Shaun Maloy – Thanks for your guidance. You were literally an answer to prayer! Keep manifesting!

To all of the professionals I worked with on this project – I can't thank you enough for your time and expertise. I'm amazed at the work that goes into publishing a book. This has truly been an eye-opening experience.

Last but certainly not the least on my list is Strategic Diversity, L.L.C. – This is the first of many projects! I look forward to publishing the next one!

DEDICATION

I dedicate my first book to you, Arlette Lanae Willis, for two special reasons. More than 20 years ago, you gave me a journal as a gift and encouraged me to write. You also prayed for me and proclaimed the Word and promises of God over me. You inspired me to believe in myself and be assured that what I have to say matters. I know your friendship has been an integral part of me being the woman I am today. Continue inspiring others to be *Transformed!*

To Daisy Darnell, even though you are no longer here on Earth, you are alive and well with God and in my heart. I truly appreciate your love, strength, and encouragement. Thank you for being the best god mother to me and grandmother to my children. We love and miss you!

And to my beautiful mother Veronica, you are a woman so worthy of being unconditionally loved and cherished. Though you didn't always experience it here on Earth, I'm so glad you are now immersed in the *real* love of your eternal life. Rest well sweet one. Rest well!

TABLE OF CONTENTS

INTRODUCTION

Love Conversations: *Christian Perspectives about Love and Relationships,* as a project, started as a way to assist people with learning more about what has been a mystery to many – how to have positive dating and marriage relationships. But it began as a means of finding out more about myself, what I want in life; and, what it means to truly be myself whenever I'm in a relationship with someone else romantically. When I started this journey, I thought I was unique in my pursuit, but I soon learned that this challenge was not uncommon. There were others who are as interested in having bold conversations about relationships, learning who they really are *and* what they truly want in relationships.

In the Christian community, people aren't always open about what they want, or what they feel about relationships because, for them, it's not the right thing to think, say or feel. My goal in writing this book is to share real and honest perspectives about love and relationships along with some of the challenges we've faced. My desire is that I somehow help someone else out there who's wondering if there are others that have similar thoughts, concerns, hopes, and dreams.

We all know that relationships are complex and can look entirely different based on the people involved so there is no magic wand or silver bullet to winning at love. The point here is, we have to be open and willing to put in the effort to have the love conversation. Are you ready to start? Good! Let's Go!

CHAPTER 1

WHY ARE YOU DATING? ARE YOU JUST HAVING FUN OR PLANNING A FUTURE?

This question is a serious one to consider before you date, and certainly when you've been dating the same person for a while. People typically have a plan before they turn the key in the ignition of their car; they know what place they are driving to and the route they intend to take. The same is true of love relationships. You (should) at least know if you are dating with the intentions of finding a person to marry, or to just enjoy a relationship without marriage being the end goal.

You can tell the difference between someone who is just in the relationship for fun, and someone dating you because they see a future with you. The latter will talk about what they see in your lives together AND begin to plan for those things to happen. You won't have to figure out if their intentions are to marry you, plan a family together, create a business together, etc. They will make it plain by their words coupled with their actions. It's essential that you recognize this important fact.

I interviewed Robert on this topic, and he shared his thoughts on how to tell if a person is dating you just for fun, or because they want a future together. Here is what he said:

The difference that I've noticed is that you are talking about what you desire in your future together even while you are having fun. They will say things like, "let's not date anyone else." They will do things to see the real you and allow themselves the opportunity to make a decision about who you are and if marriage is a real possibility based on compatibility. For example, getting involved with family situations to see if that dynamic is what they really want to deal with. If your partner won't let you meet their family, that's a red flag." As a side note, Robert said he also used his dating time to see if his girlfriend (now wife) upheld his values as a Christian believer. *He said, "A person that wants to test your beliefs is not really for you. They should want to support you in your Christian walk. They won't want to hamper you.*

I recently listened to a pastor talk about the difference between a man looking for a girlfriend and one looking for a wife. He said,

> "*A man that is looking for a wife dates for that purpose and is clear about his intentions. Once he determines that you are* <u>his wife</u>, *he will begin treating you as if you are, even if he hasn't asked you to marry him yet. He will make sure you are safe, that your car is filled with gas (that he has paid for), and that you are ok emotionally, physically and spiritually. He will treat you with respect and will do what he has to do to win your heart – even if that means waiting for you for a specific period of time. A man interested in a girlfriend will not wait for you or protect you (financially, spiritually or otherwise); nor will he sacrifice to the point of personal inconvenience. He will primarily pursue a girlfriend to the point of personal gain – nothing more.*"

To support his perspective, the pastor's wife talked about how he sacrificed time and money to ensure he spent time with her, although she lived in another state. He protected her heart and their relationship by refraining from putting her in a compromising position. He treated her son from a previous relationship as if he were his own, long before they married. They had the tough conversations about their pasts and what they wanted for the future. They prayed together and shared their hearts with one another. He acted like a husband, not a boyfriend, which made it easy for her to trust her heart to him in marriage.

And that brings up a good point here for us to all consider. A man or woman that has a "boyfriend/girlfriend" mindset will focus primarily on the present, their feelings and fun times. Trust me. If they ever talk about the future at all, they will talk only about *their* goals, dreams and plans. They will steer clear of discussions related to planning a future together as husband and wife. If you ask them where things are going in the relationship, they'll tell you things like, "Let's see where this goes" or "I'm not sure". If they ever discuss the future with you, it will only be when you bring it up and be sure the response from them will be very vague and ambiguous, leaving you in a state of confusion. That feeling of being "unsure" will remain the theme of your relationship if they aren't truly interested in marrying you.

Please don't get me wrong. Being sure is very important; taking the time to know what each of you wants is an important step before you pledge your life and fidelity to one another. However, if all they want to offer you is a fun time, you have to consider the options. If your goal is just to have fun, then enjoy the companionship. But if you want something deeper and committed, then wake up to the reality of what they are really willing to offer. If it doesn't suit your plan of having a committed relationship, move on with your life and find a pasture where the grasses are greener. There is someone out there who wants to seal that commitment in their heart with a wedding ring. Like Beyoncé said in one of her songs, "If you liked it then you shoulda put a ring on it!"

CHAPTER 2

A HAPPY SINGLE LIFE IS THE FOUNDATION FOR A GOOD MARRIED LIFE

"People accept the love they think they deserve."

– The Perks of Being a Wildflower

A few years ago, I asked a recently divorced friend about dating. She had been divorced for a few years before starting to see other people again. While we talked about how dating was going, I asked, "Were you happy before you dated?" She told me that there were times when she needed to be held, and needed someone's shoulders to lean on, but there was no one there to offer help or solutions for her challenges. Even though that was the case, she was however happy being single. It felt good spending time doing the things that she enjoyed doing, like investing in her education and spending time with her family and friends. Della's relationship with God and her local church were important to her, and she spent time connecting with her pastors and with other believers. She also enjoyed the extra time she had for mentoring young people in her community and being with her sorority sisters. Ask anyone around about her, and they'll tell you Della is brilliant, an expert in her field, and one of the best friends a person could ask for. Della is pretty awesome!

One of the things she said that struck me was that she was *content before dating,* so dating only added to her experience. She enjoyed the dates that didn't go anywhere because she had a good time. Dating was an experience for her and not a contact sport.

I asked her what she was looking for in a future relationship, and I tell you, her expectations were simple. She was looking for a "grown man" to love and build a life together with. She knew that rushing to be in a relationship would be a major mistake. She wanted a marriage that would stand the test of time. Since she knew it would take "time" to connect with the right person, she waited. Being in a state of contentment and wholeness of mind allowed her to focus on what was important in her life and not get side-tracked. And that's a perfect place to be.

Not too many years after this conversation, she met and married a wonderful man. They complement one another very well and they both love their families. They spend quality time in their relationships with friends and the community.

What is most impressive about him is how he showed and maintained his love and commitment for her during a particularly hard time in her life. While they were dating, Della became very sick. Now, it is very typical of some men to run away when confronted with the challenges she was faced with, but he wasn't one of those typical men. He made it his business to love her through it thick and thin. Although his work required a lot of travel, he got on the road and drove many miles to make sure he personally took care of her. He even took vacation time to be there when she needed him. The distance and the expense didn't matter to him – she was what mattered the most to him. This "grown man" pursued her heart by doing the *work of love* (because love is a verb) just like she did for others before coming into a relationship with him. He showed her the willingness and commitment typical of "husband material" by acting like her husband before he married her. This was the desire of her heart, and it sure did come to pass.

I'm glad I could witness this before and after singleness journey. It shows why it is the best route to take in life when you wait to know yourself, stay focused on the important things in your life, and when you wait on God.

CHAPTER 3

THE PROCESS

What the Pursuit Means:

The act of following in an effort to capture

There is a process that happens before you say "I Do." This process involves pursuing (and being pursued) and dating, to name a few. The topic of pursuit is often discussed in the church. But, what does it really mean? How does it relate to and affect you as an individual?

Being pursued by a man in a love/relationship-related sense is very important to many women. Some time ago, I asked a group of women about why being pursued is important to them, and they all echoed the same answer; a man's efforts to win her heart places value on the relationship; his efforts mean she is worth it, and that he is willing to do what he needs to do to win her love and keep her heart.

Pursuing a woman may have little or nothing to do with bringing home a paycheck or paying the bills, especially if she is financially independent. Pursuing her in a sexual manner isn't a great value either, because sex is an easy commodity to obtain. The culture that is trending now is all about having meaningless sex. If you don't believe me, listen to the popular hip-hop song "In Da Club" by hip-hop artist 50 Cent. It says, *"...I'm into havin' sex. I ain't into makin' love so come give me a hug if you're into gettin' rubbed"*. "Pause" by Pop artist Pitbull says, *"Mamita would you play? And if you say ok, we will play night and day. I'm such a dirty, dirty dog; my teeth will unsnap your bra but for now baby just pause"*. Here's another song by country singer Eric Church. The song, 'Like a Wrecking Ball' says, *"...That whole house is going to be shaking. I hope those bricks and boards can take it. I want to rock some sheetrock and some pictures off the wall. I'm gonna rock you baby like a wrecking ball."*

Hold on. Before you judge 50 Cent, Pitbull or Eric Church too harshly, I have heard similarities in just about every genre of music. And for those who're ready to point accusing fingers at the secular world, let's be very honest, you can find this same mindset sitting in the pews of our local churches. Sex is easy to get.

Now that we've established that money and sex aren't the greatest values in pursuit, what is?

The purest value that happens as a result of pursuit is an eye-opening recognition for the person you are with. This eye-opening comes from continually seeking to know who she is, and truly recognizing the value of the emotional and intellectual intimacy she shares with you. This happens when you stay engaged in the relationship and refrain from things go into "autopilot." It's also about having "godly pride" in who she is and letting her know it by what you say and what you do. Pursuit pushes you into letting her know she is priceless. It helps you as the man who's pursuing her place a high value of her in your heart. It's like saying to yourself, "She's different, she's priceless, and she would add value to a good man's life. I am that good man for her!"

Ever wonder why a simple-looking man has a beautiful and brilliant woman at his side? He may have mastered the art and act of getting to know her heart, and pursuing and treasuring her.

Don't ever underestimate the power of pursuit.

How long should we date before... THE BIG QUESTION?

"Will you marry me?"

That's a tricky question, right? If you Google this question, hundreds of articles will appear with different perspectives on how long it should take before you ask, or how long before you should expect to hear the big question. Like many writers will do, I can't really tell you how many days, months, or even years you should wait. But I will tell you that the waiting time should be one that is agreed upon by both parties. Once the timeframe is established, you can use that time to learn everything about that person and yourself in the process.

I once asked Ethan, a young man in his early 20s, who has traveled to several countries in the past few years, about his thoughts on how long a person should wait before the big question. I think you'll agree he is a pretty mature young man. Here is what he said:

I think you should wait more than a year and a half. The timeframe will vary for each person in the relationship, but it will allow them time to learn who the other person is, their secrets and whether or not they can deal with them. If you are with them for less than a year and a half, it doesn't allow you time to know who they are or allow them to come out of their shell. It takes time to see what they do in certain situations. You can think that person is the nicest person in the world, but people tend to show you who they really are after time. Usually, within a year, everyone will have something tragic happen in their lives and you get to see what they are like under pressure. When you are with someone, you have to see who he or she is when tragedies strike, because people often change to cope with hard situations. You have to determine whether or not you can deal with that person when things are difficult. When you are in the honeymoon phase of dating, you may think your lover is wonderful, but after the honeymoon phase is over, you may find out they are self-centered, bad with money, passive, aggressive or worse – emotionally or physically abusive.

The discussion further confirms our previous discussion about taking your time before rushing in. You should definitely take the time to get to know the person at all times and in any season of life. You should be well acquainted with their strengths and flaws. Deciding who your marriage partner will be isn't about finding someone who is flawless, but rather about finding someone whose strengths and flaws you can live with. If marriage is on the horizon, ensure that you undertake a series of wise pre-marital counseling. The truth is, every relationship has tough times. Your counseling then should be focused on how to make the marriage work when things go wrong. Don't allow your pursuit of getting to the altar to tie the knot overshadow the fact that when the wedding is over, you will have to live with this person for the rest of your existence. My advice? Take your time honey. Take your time!

Another question you should ask as you date is, "What do I really want?" And then, "Is this person willing and able to give it to me?" I've had countless conversations with some of my male and female friends who intend to get married; they want to have children, build a business, and travel with their spouses. But the unfortunate thing here is, while they crave to have all of these achieved in the relationship with their dating partner, some don't show a similar interest. They just want to wait around and watch how things go. When it comes down to really committing to them, they shy away or shut down entirely.

Most of the time, they are caught between two worlds. On the one hand, they are in love and want to spend their time forever with their significant other. On the other hand, they know deep within that they will miss out on all of the other things they want out of life if they choose to remain in the relationship. One cannot help but ask, "Did they ever talk about what they wanted out of the relationship up front?" Yes, they did. But in many cases, the other party preferred to pretend and not ruin a good thing by telling the truth so they lead them on. In the end, they felt satisfied with what they are getting out of the relationship and gave little thought to the misery their partner experienced.

I once read an article about a woman who experienced a similar issue. She was in a relationship with someone who was great for the moment, but in the long run, wasn't interested in investing in a long-term commitment and relationship. Though she loved him deeply, she realized she'd made the mistake of choosing a man that loved himself more than he loved her.

If you are in the same boat with her, I won't tell you which of the routes to take, because it is simply a matter of the heart. But I'll advise you not to stay with someone who doesn't value you, who ultimately disregards your desire to be married, have a family, or whatever your need is in life. You'll only find yourself disappointed in the long run. That's never a good foundation to build a healthy life on.

Don't ever walk in fear that the relationship you are in is the only one you'll ever have. It's just a misconception. There is something beautiful waiting for you beyond the fear.

Part of the process includes choosing the right relationship. But, what does that look like? The other part of it is knowing what character you play.

In any relationship, there are two main characters: confident and dependent. The confident one is that self-assured individual who is looking for a mate that will complement and support their faith, family and career goals. They always desire to have someone who will be with them through thick and thin. This personality type is looking to give love, and also desires to have a partner that will reciprocate the same.

They are internally driven and do not rely on external stimuli to drive them towards reaching their God-ordained destiny. They aren't quitters – they are fighters, and that is what they are looking for in a mate.

On the other hand, you have the dependent one. This person relies on someone else for fulfilment and to find joy. This personality is slick, and you can't always tell who this person is at first glance until you carefully take time to study him or her patiently. A woman who belongs in this category may seem to want your input in *every* area of her life. Do you like this dress? Am I pretty? What should do? These are things she may want to seek your opinion on. She may seem to hang on your every word. Her desire to place every decision into her man's hands may be quite flattering at first - that is until she can't seem to make her own decisions. If it really came down to it and you needed her help, she couldn't coach you out of an open paper bag.

Have you ever seen the movie *Coming to America*? If you haven't, check it out! It's hilarious! One of the most unforgettable moments in the movie is a scene where a beautiful voluptuous woman, raised from infancy to meet the special desires of her fiancé, finally encounters her soon-to-be husband (the Prince) for the first time. When I say "every desire," I mean she is taught to know, like and do whatever he likes, at the expense of her pursuing her own personal choices. Now guys, I know you're thinking, "Hey! What's wrong with that?!" Right? Just keep following the story.

The Prince asked her a simple question, "What do you like?" That's a simple and basic question, right? Her response? "Whatever you like." The Prince was disappointed by her answer. He tried encouraging her to express her own opinions and intelligence, but it all fell on deaf ears as she keeps telling him "Whatever you like." Though she is drop-dead gorgeous, the prince found her completely unsuitable for him.

Beauty has its place no doubt, but she couldn't function beyond a small segment of a beauty contest, because beauty pageants require more than just aesthetics. He knew he couldn't lean on her in times of trouble because she depended solely on him for survival. He'd have better luck with asking Google or Amazon Alexa devices for advice than seeking her counsel.

In the end, the Prince found, pursued, and won the heart of an independent woman who could share his challenge, help develop his intellect and rule his kingdom. You can never get that from a Ms Dependent. I'm just sayin'!

Now, Mr Dependent can be an interesting person to figure out too, so you ladies have got to watch out. A friend who recently came across this kind of personality said it was quite devastating for her when she discovered Mr Right wasn't who she thought he was. She recalled some of the things he would always say, like "A woman can get a man to open up and be so much more if she encouraged him more," or some self-effacing statements like, "I'm really not all that attractive."

Now, ladies, you may be thinking, "Oh this is great! He's so humble. I can help build him up to be the man I want him to be". Don't fool yourself. You may have to inflate his ego to keep the relationship going consistently. At any time you disagree with him on a particular issue, he may shut down on you because he feels the disagreement will affect his manhood.

This kind of relationship requires an ego-boosting "Yes Woman"; a woman who only says and does things that are agreeable to the man. You'll need to throw those years of wisdom and discernment out the door to keep Mr Dependent happy. Are you ready for that kind of life? I'm sure you readily have a NO answer.

Dependent men can in many ways, use the conquest of a certain kind of woman as his way of feeling good about himself. An older man may seek a younger woman just because she is young, and he probably needs her to make him feel better about himself. Associating with younger women makes him feel somehow youthful. A dependent, younger man may seek to get into relationships with older women because he thinks she is better intellectually, financially, or has a certain status. Being with her, to him, makes him feel better about himself and complements his weakness.

You'll notice, in both examples, the drive to get the woman has more to do with what she represents (like her age, beauty, status or achievements) and little or nothing to do with who the woman is herself. He can boast about her physical appearance, wealth, and status as bonuses for himself, but like the book of Proverbs 27:20 (MSG) says, *"Hell has a voracious appetite, and lust just never quits."* What this simply translates to mean is that he will never get enough from a woman, but will keep moving from one to another for lustful satisfaction. This will lead him to always seek someone younger, more beautiful, more connected, more mature – just MORE! Like someone once told me, "men love the chase."

He will continue to sabotage relationships, including the good ones, because he is perpetually searching. His searching will ultimately cause him to by-pass the woman who is best for him. The holes in his life will make him keep looking for the wrong things in his mate. This will lead to total confusion because he will be lost in life regarding to what he wants for himself.

Are you getting the message from all of these stories? As you consider where you are on the relationship spectrum, please remember that it's important for you to have worked on yourself before bringing someone into your life. You'll prevent catastrophes down the road when you get to know your issues, and seek guidance and healing from God before engaging someone else. If you don't deal with the real issues, I'm afraid you may continue to look for fillers (people) in the areas of your life that only God can fill. And in the end, you'll remain empty, broken, disgusted, and disappointed. And just like a black hole, you will suck up and destroy anything that comes into your path. I'm sure you don't want this kind of life.

There are many benefits that accrue to us when we take the time to know ourselves. First off, it allows us to truly settle in our hearts what we really want for ourselves in life. When you have a confident mindset about what you want out of life, you'll definitely be on the lookout for things that will complement it, in your mate. Anyone that doesn't fit the model won't be your choice. A confident woman who wants to have a man that loves and commits himself to her, won't settle for the guy who only wants to offer part-time lover status. It won't matter to her if he has the body of Morris Chestnut or Channing Tatum.

The same is true for men. A confident man seeking a good wife won't settle for the girl whose only value is how "hot" she is to him and perhaps, to other guys. He'll always desire to find a partner that will complement him.

The second benefit attached to knowing ourselves is that it helps us build and accumulate a vast amount of personal experience to draw from. When we invest quality time in self-improvement, travel, reading, networking, fellowshipping and serving others, we are better able to relate to the world and understand how others think and feel. What this does is help us shape our viewpoints and ultimately allows us to better relate to our future mates.

A person that takes the time to learn and experience new things also shows a high level of self-care and self-respect. It sends a clear signal to others about how you expect them to treat you. If we lack value for ourselves, we will ultimately teach others to disrespect us. It's as simple as that.

My brother and I were discussing this book, and I asked him for words of advice. And he said something I won't ever forget. He said, "Fill Your Own Cup. Don't look for someone else to make you complete. Stand tall and know your own worth." Simple, but powerful I'll say.

The fact is, a man or woman who knows who they are and what they want, will be more attractive, compared to a person who is needy, clingy and requiring someone other than God to make them feel whole.

Before I started dating again, I didn't do this important internal work. I honestly didn't seek to understand who I was and what made me truly happy and complete. I was deeply hurt within, and my main goal was to stop the pain. Unfortunately, what that resulted in was a lot of heartaches and wasted time. Reality dawned on me later, and I found myself asking, "What have I done?" Why was I ever with that guy? Or in the words of Tyler Perry's character Madea, "What in the hell was I thinking?!" It was like waking up with a severe hangover after a night of serious drinking. The difference here is that mine was a severe internal hangover all because I didn't take the valuable time to get to know myself.

When I came to myself, I started focusing on my inner struggles and what was causing me to make the choices I was making. I began to recognize my own vicious cycles and took steps to deal with the truth about them. It was after then that I began to understand my own worth, the real truth about who I am, who God says I am, and what I want from life. Once that was done, I stopped accepting everything that came my way. I refused to accept behaviors that were toxic to me, and I started declaring openly what is important in my life.

Life has been very different for me since I chose this part. And believe me, I'm continually amazed at the beautiful things that have been happening in my life since I made the change.

Friends, in a nutshell, before you pursue or allow yourself to be pursued, you've got to know the real "you." Getting comfortable with the person on the inside helps you know the value you bring to the table, and it helps you to identify the qualities you and your future partner will need, to have a lasting, mature and fulfilling relationship. Confident pursuers are better positioned to win the love game.

CHAPTER 4

TIME FOR MARRIAGE

Why I want to Get Married!

"If I get married, I want to be very married."

– Audrey Hepburn

As a little girl, the idea of rushing down the aisle and living happily ever after was the stuff fairy tales were made of. Many of us still hold that idea. On the other hand, many of us have seen the effects of marriage and have a variety of perspectives on why we do or do not want to be married. I asked a few friends why they want to be married or why they don't, and here's what one of them said.

"I love the idea and God's design for marriage."

My friend Sasha is a gorgeous woman in her 40s. She was once married, divorced, and now single. She's accomplished career-wise and has it going in many areas of life. I asked her why she's still interested in getting married again, and she shared this with me.

I've been divorced for three years now. I love the idea and God's design for marriage. I love the design of two people coming together as one. As a single woman, I am wonderful, but I am an incomplete portion of the human experience. I feel men have an incomplete portion of the human experience as well. Men have certain perspectives, abilities and skills sets that I don't possess as a woman. Two people (male and female) coming together brings both portions of the human experience together. I still want children, and I don't want them outside of marriage. The financial stability that comes along with marriage is also a pro.

Me: *That's great Sasha but in a perfect world job loss happens. What would you do if your husband lost his job?*

Sasha: *I would want a person who has a mindset that if the financial situations change, this is only a temporary situation. He would have the mindset to get out and start a business or hustle up on something to make sure he stays in the mindset of providing for his family. In the meantime, we are partners so I would hold us down until that changes.*

Me: *Tell me what else you are looking for in your future husband.*

Sasha: *I'm also looking for someone on the same level, mentally, physically, financially and culturally – we have to be equally yoked. I need to have someone who has experienced things that I have, or that is willing to experience them with me.*

Since Sasha had been married before, I wanted to know what things she had learned in her previous marriage that she would love to bring into a new marriage.

I've learned who I am and therefore I will be more honest about my expectations for my future husband. I've also learned that marriage is work and knowing that, I desire to be with the right person more than just being married. Initially, I wanted to be married more than being focused on the person I married – this is why I glossed over things I saw were real problems early on.

Sasha's ex-husband had a problem that affected them financially, and due to this, she was left with the responsibility of taking care of the family. She automatically became the breadwinner of the family. She felt bitter about it, and this eventually turned into disrespect for her husband. Here's what she learned:

> *I learned that I should never emasculate my husband because I learned that no matter what, I'm responsible for showing respect to my husband even if he does things that aren't right. This is another human being that I share intimate space with and the words I use against him can cut deep. I am responsible for what comes out of my mouth. I realize that when I'm at work, and my boss says or does something I don't like, I can't storm into their office and say whatever I want because that wouldn't go well for me. Likewise, I am responsible for treating my husband with the same level of respect and more. That's one of the things I have learned and will give my husband in the future.*

My friend Michelle is a soft and kind reflection of love. She's an educator and a trusted friend. She is in her mid-40s and hasn't been married yet. I asked her why she wanted to get married and here are her reasons:

I want companionship and romance. I want to experience romantic love within a holy marriage. I also want to have male support for the life's challenges. I feel as though I've been gifted with so much love that I want to give. I want to be a lover and a companion to someone else that desires the same things. She paused a little and asked, *Does that sound selfish?*

Me: (A bit surprised) *No. Why did you ask?*

Michelle: *I read a number of Christian books that said your desire for marriage should primarily be to further God's kingdom. Anything outside of that is wrong.*

Me: *I think marriage is supposed to be a representation of the love God has for the church. It's all about being there no matter what, loving in the good and hard times, being present and witnessing the life of your spouse, planning together, growing together AND, should you decide to do so, having children and raising a family together. I've heard some people say marriage is just for reproduction, but a marriage that is relegated to mere reproduction doesn't represent the love that Christ has for the church - not at all.*

Michelle: *Though I wanted to have babies, I'm beyond the stage of having children. Parts of me want to be a nurturer – that's a desire I have – I have a desire to give my love and take care of someone else and help meet someone else's needs. I would want to be with someone that would consider adoption because I want to have a family unit that would consist of more than just me and him. I'm looking for a best friend. I desire someone who loves God, who has integrity, a sense of humor and is not so spiritually minded that he can't be real. I'm looking for someone who is loyal, will make me laugh and someone who's good at giving (not selfish) – and someone who is supportive of my own personal goals and not try to stifle me in the pursuits I have in my life. I want someone who will push me to be better.*

Though Michelle has never been married, she has dated in the past. I wanted to know what she learned as a result of previous relationships and what nuggets of wisdom she'd bring to the table. Here's what she has to say:

I've learned that having a relationship with someone is not worth compromising my authentic self or my values. I compromised so much just to have companionship and love from somebody. I've always felt like I had to compromise who I am to have it – be someone else in order to have them. I've done that, and it has never been worth it. I've learned valuing myself is one of the best things I can bring to a relationship because if I don't value myself, I won't be able to truly receive the love that he will have for me or love him the way he will need to be loved. I think we love based on how we feel about ourselves.

Marriage: "...it's just not my thing." Two Millennial Perspectives

"If you were my husband, I'd poison your tea!"

"If you were my wife, I'd drink it."

— Lady Astor and Winston Churchill

As much as I love marriage, I do understand however that not everyone wants to be married. That may sound strange to some, but it's true: marriage may not be for everyone.

I asked a few people why they wanted to get married, and I got very interesting perspectives some I didn't quite expect. I asked 22-year old Natasha about her intentions as it relates to marriage, and she surprised me with this reply:

To be honest, at this point in my life, someone would have to convince me that marriage is a good thing. I feel very cautious when my friends talk about marriage. They think more about bachelorette parties, wedding ceremonies or babies. I usually get quiet because I think of sacrifice and someone getting on my nerves. I would have to be convinced that this is a person I'm willing to be with. I'm terrified of getting married to somebody that I'm not supposed to be married to. I have not been exposed to many examples of a good marriage, so that has tainted my perception of what marriage is.

Natasha's parents are divorced. Unfortunately, she saw things happen in their marriage that deter the idea of marriage as a viable option for her.

I asked another millennial, Jazz by name, about her perspective on marriage. Read her perspective below.

I don't want to be tied down to anyone legally. I don't want to take part in issues that come up legally, like the person not paying their taxes, or other things that happen financially that you become responsible for. I don't want to be tied down to that.

Divorce is really frowned upon, but in my experience, people drag a marriage out unnecessarily. They say it's for the children when it really isn't. They don't know the effect an unhealthy marriage has on the kids. Of course, you don't want to get a divorce, but you shouldn't be unhappy either. Overall, I think marriage can be a good thing, and if my friends want to be married I will support them, but it's just not my thing.

While being married is something that a lot of people desire, it's important to understand that it isn't a cure for all issues. Marriage doesn't solve all of our problems. One of those issues is loneliness. It's something else, isn't it? There was once a time I used to think that loneliness could be cured by external things. I later found this to be untrue, and in fact, you can try surrounding yourself with family, friends and significant others, and still feel lonely.

I thought the constant companionship would fill the empty space I had in my life, but I soon learned the truth. You can be married and still be lonely. You can share almost everything and sleep in the same bed, and still feel absolutely alone.

As I lay in my bed one night, I noticed how sore my arm was. I had moved a bunch of boxes, and I pulled a muscle. I also noticed how sore my heart was; I was sore from being alone - needing and wanting to be held and appreciated but not having that need fulfilled. A need every functioning human on the planet earth will have.

The need for companionship is not just an idea; it can be scientifically proved. There have been studies about child development and human nurturing. One of such studies compared the growth and development of children placed in an environment where they were only being fed, clothed, had their diapers changed, and bathed. Another group of children was held, cuddled, talked to and played with in addition to being fed, changed and bathed. Which of the two groups would you think thrived the most? Your guess was right! The children that received nurturing.

I was listening to Fred Hammond's CD "God, Love and Romance" some time ago. One of his songs titled "Easier" profoundly sums up the feeling of loneliness. The song is about a person caught between the paradox of being lonely and the fear of reconnecting with someone new and being hurt. The lyrics go this way; *"A lonely heart gets cold too soon, and the one will be much colder than two - colder than a winter night in June."* It further goes on to say; *"Maybe we'll just be friends, but it's easier than being alone, easier than dying, easier than crying, easier than living without you."* The need to be connected is normal. But the question is, "How do you deal with loneliness while you wait?"

As I said earlier, the best way to deal with loneliness is taking time to understand your triggers, hurts, and expectations. This is important because understanding what lies beneath the surface helps you discern where the lonely feelings are coming from. Once you do that, you'll be able to deal with loneliness from a healthy perspective. Loneliness may be a symptom of a much bigger issue. Putting Band-Aids on things that need open-heart surgery won't do the trick. The good news is this isn't something you have to handle alone. Sharing with friends or family who can relate, is so important. In my experiences, I learned the benefits of sharing the things I'd gone through with my friends and family.

I digress here for a moment. Let's be clear; I'm not talking about sharing your internal struggles with leaky, unwise, or judgmental people. No. I have a saying, *"If you can't hold water in a glass, you certainly can't handle me."* More specifically, *"If you leak everyone else's business, I'm certainly not telling you anything about mine."* Leaky "friends" are easy to spot. You'll know who they are from the things they tell you about others. If they tell you something personal about others, be sure they'll certainly tell others personal things about you. Be discerning. You should answer all questions about how you are doing with, "Great! How are you?"

The next thing you can do to deal with loneliness is to serve others. The Bible talks about how a single person, unlike a married one, can focus on serving the Lord (See I Corinthians 7:32) this, however, comprises a lot of things and not necessarily just serving in the church. You can spend time mentoring young people, helping families in your neighborhood or serving community programs like "Forgotten Harvest." You could also use whatever gifts or talents you have to help others. Some sections of this book, for example, were written while I was in a lonely place.

You can also spend time traveling and meeting new people locally and globally. Yes, people! It's a big world out there, and there are more than 7.6 billion people on planet Earth. Think about the great experiences and opportunities you are missing.

Now before you say, "I don't have anyone to go with me", it will interest you to know that I traveled alone when I had my first trip to another country. Yes, I did it all by myself! I boarded a plane and went to the Dominican Republic by myself. I wanted to go with friends, but they all, for one reason or the other, couldn't go with me. I decided I wasn't going to put my dream on hold because I was single or because my friends had other plans. No, I got on a plane and went anyway. And you know what? I met people; on the plane; on the resort; in restaurants and everywhere else I visited. I had a blast! I learned some Spanish along the way because people took the time to teach me. My Spanish caused a few comical moments, but I learned and had a great time doing it. And you know what? I still keep in contact with a few people I met there.

The point in all of this is to use your time as a single person wisely and enjoy it to the fullest! Believe me; there are a few married people out there who wish they'd wisely maximized the days when they were single. You don't have to have that same story.

Equally Yoked: To Be or Not to Be? – That is The Question.

"Marry your equally-yoked best friend! It will save you from meeting up with a complete stranger in divorce court".

– Anonymous

We (often) date with the purpose of marrying. But, should we date someone who doesn't share our faith if marriage is the goal?

I've heard many say, "Don't date or pursue a person that doesn't have saving faith in Jesus Christ." I don't disagree – necessarily. I think I'll add to that and say, *"Don't date or pursue anyone who doesn't exhibit the love of God either."* Hey! Just because a person claims to be a Christian doesn't mean that they are actually walking out the "love" principle...I'm just sayin!

Being unequally yoked goes much deeper than just your faith. Just because someone shares your faith in God does not mean they are the one for you. The "faith" question is the ticket into the dance. The question then becomes, "Can they dance with you?" You may want to know what I mean by that. I'll tell you.

I've learned a few things about myself that have really helped me recognize what type of person is best for me. I've learned that I adore people who genuinely love being involved in the lives and affairs of others – people who show genuine care towards others. People who always find the motivation to serve the needs of others.

I don't like judgmental or rigid people. The thoughts of being with a man who will use the Bible as a sword in our relationship to hurt me always scares me. I adore humor and intelligence, but I don't like overly sarcastic and mean people or intelligent snobs. Men who name-drop all of the time make my skin crawl. Open, honest, and respectful communication is one of my love languages. A man who is dismissive of the feelings of others or avoids conflict wouldn't be a good fit either.

With that being said, just being a person that shares my faith in God doesn't mean that I'll find the guy attractive, or that he will make a good mate for me. Hey! Even if a person is a total package, that doesn't mean they are a package that I need to keep.

The fact is, we all know a lot of people who claim to be Christians by name, but are abusive, manipulative, controlling and full of anger. Yes, they can jump and shout you up and down the church isles, quote the Bible from Genesis to Revelations and pray the mountaintops down. In fact, they may have an official title in the church. But if they have personal characteristics that are toxic, the relationship will be painful. It's their character that you'll live with. We need to evaluate people well beyond the idea of sharing the same faith, to know whether or not we are equally yoked.

It is pertinent to note that, part of finding our equally-yoked partner is also asking ourselves whether or not the person is a good man or woman. But, what does that really mean? Who exactly is a good man or woman? Who gets to define that?

If you read fashion magazines or go on social media, a good man has a six-pack, can lift an elephant with a single hand, has a chiseled face and can break a walnut with his butt cheeks. A good man is a fine man according to their definition. And, if you look at the Wall Street Journal, a good man is a wealthy one. He can buy and sell anything or anyone for that matter. He's got his financial act together. Some may see a good man as a brilliant one with an IQ in the 200 range.

If we take pop culture's views, many amazing men will end up on the losing side of what the society defines as a good man. Let's see a few comments from people on who a good man or woman really is.

I asked my single friend Nicole for her idea of what a good man is. Nicole has never been married, so I really wanted to get her thoughts about this concept.

A good man believes in the Lord, lives his life for the Lord, has faith and is faithful. He's led by the Lord, hard-working, intelligent, treats himself and others well, open to new experiences and expresses himself well. Having a man with these qualities makes me feel safe and at ease.

Me: *What have those characteristics meant to you?*

Nicole: *I'm not sure I'm the right person to answer that question.*

Me: *Why?*

Nicole: *I didn't grow up with a man in my life to show love to me. I didn't have a dad, brothers or uncles. I don't have a frame of reference. I guess these qualities show self-love, and maybe the guy can show that love to others.*

Next up is Rhonda, a funny, highly educated, beautiful women. She's a mother of one and recently remarried. Here are her thoughts.

> *There are all sorts of qualities. Each man is different. A few requirements include intelligence, empathy, emotional maturity and a sense of humor. I just want him to be a good person. A good man would love the way he supposed to. I like to be loved passionately and consistently.*

This next perspective is coming from a younger woman. She's 17 and in her junior year in high school. Karen is highly respected by her friends for being mature for her age. I really wanted to see what she thought about the "good man" questions.

> Karen: *For me, being considerate of people's feelings makes a good man. He has to have good home training. Boys sometimes act like their parents didn't teach them anything. Huh! Maybe they didn't.*
>
> *He has to be saved (a Christian believer). I really want one of those. He has to have goals, be funny, attractive and tall. I can't do the short (guy) thing – I can't do it!! He also has to be committed and loyal to*

the relationship. He has to treat me like I'm important and be someone I can be myself around with. He has to be someone who respects me. Those qualities would make me feel important because...I don't know...it would make me feel like I'm one-in-a-million...like....I'm special and not like any other girl he's dated and stuff.

Here's what 21-year-old Jazz had to say about the makings of a good man.

While growing up, I saw bad examples. I think that he has to be....hmm... emotionally intact. A lot of men grow up being encouraged to only express anger. They are not encouraged to express sadness or other emotions. Um! So I need him to be able to hear me say I'm upset about something and have the ability to empathize rather than say, "You're crazy" or "I don't understand why you are upset". That's very important to me. His ability to express his emotions about things that bother him or that make him happy is important. Besides the emotional stuff, I want him to be supportive of women's equality. The men in my family have traditional views. They think, "I am the man. Hear me roar!", "I make the decisions" and "What I say goes". That bothers me a lot. Despite those attitudes, I come from a family of women who are very opinionated, so having a man who views women as equals is important.

Humor is important to me because I like to laugh. I'm pretty goofy, so having a guy with humor is important. What's also important to me is intelligence. I can't have conversations with someone who is very dull. I want someone who has a basic understanding of things and who can teach me something – just be smart. I would definitely appreciate a man like that and be grateful that I got a good one.

To balance the equation, I took time to engage men about the "good woman" question too.

When you look at it, the good woman is carefully defined by the society as a combination of Beyoncé Knowles and Mary Poppins. She's got a banging body though she's had multiple babies, takes meticulous care of her family, has an amazing career and can make her man feel like A REAL MAN at all times – all without help or skipping a single beat. A good woman is a Superwoman!

I don't know about you, but many women, though awesome in their own right, may not fit into society's "good woman" definition.

I asked my friend Andrew, a recently married man in his 40s, about his views on what makes a good woman and what that would mean to him.

Personally, I think a good woman is somebody who stands up for her beliefs. Someone who is willing to sacrifice for the sake of love; a person who is compassionate and has her own individuality. She wants you, but she still has her own views and opinions. For me, a good woman is a woman that would uplift me in word and in deed. She is someone who is willing to learn about me. Someone who loves me. She is someone who loves the Lord. She has to love God first – even before me. I need her to love God first because then she'll put me first. A woman who already has kids must be willing to let the man help raise her children. She also has to be willing to take correction in a loving way. She will follow the leadership of her home and pass those values on to her children by teaching them positive behaviors and not enabling bad habits. A good woman will not cause division but will do things to build her home.

Reynard, a divorcee in his late 40s, gave his perspective on a good woman.

> *A good woman is someone who is loving, caring and has a good heart. She is someone who listens and helps. She's someone who isn't just concerned about herself. She is principled (meaning she knows right from wrong) and she chooses to do what's right. She's a good mother. She makes sure the kids are ok and helps her kids to grow up into fine human beings. She teaches her kids how to do things and provide for themselves. She also models how to be a good person. Knowing that I'm with this type of a person helps me to build and strengthen a bond with her.*

I asked Antonio, a 45-year-old divorcée, what he feels are the characteristics of a good woman.

> *To me, a good woman is kind, humble, has a sense of humor and shows compassion to others. She's patient, understanding, intelligent and godly. If I were with someone like this, it would make me feel at peace, happy, and loved. If you are with a person that is patient, understanding, and kind, you are dealing with a person that is willing to learn about you and love you*

as you are. It will make me feel comfortable with being myself around her. Having a sense of humor is also a big deal with me. I believe it can inject joy and playfulness into the relationship – to me there is nothing like laughing hard with the person that you love. A person that has a sense of humor can help to diffuse a situation and can help you to see the brighter side of things. As it relates to intelligence, I think having an intelligent woman in your life can help you to see things from a different viewpoint. If you are an intelligent man that is not prideful, you will see that as a huge benefit, not only for you but for your life together. I kind of look at it like this: If you were looking to put together your super team, you would put together the best people for the team. If you own a company, you look for someone who is knowledgeable and capable to partner with. We tend to look for something similar in our personal lives as well. I consider a life-long partner more important.

Me: *Do you place any weight on how she looks?*

Antonio: *I think that the appearance is one of the least important aspects. I've learned you can be physically attracted to somebody but get to know them and find there is nothing attractive about them. It's more than just a pretty smile or how she dresses because women are more than that. The truth of the matter is, the more you are with someone, the more you get used to their appearance. Once you move past the aesthetics, you focus more on the functionality of the person and whether or not it works well.*

So, you may be thinking about what my own perspectives are on the "good man" question. Here's are my thoughts: A good man is not a perfect man but one who has a heart after God, and who loves me with all of his heart. He is kind-hearted, strong, willing to lead, and also be led by God. Though solid in his thinking, a good man listens to his spouse and to those he is accountable to. He is open, passionate, funny, and wise. He has the ability to draw out the best in people and also celebrate the accomplishments of others.

A good man will love our children. It's very important for him to spend quality time with his children, love and support them, provide them with direction and a good example. I find it very attractive when a man gives time and attention to his children. Reasons for this, I cannot tell but it's really attractive to me. I would want him to love, support, and treat them with care.

A good man loves his family and friends. The way he treats his family and friends is very important to me, because it serves as an indicator of how he will treat me. If he neglects his mom, the chances are pretty high that I'll be neglected as well. If he values time with his family, he will definitely find value in spending time with mine. If he doesn't consider the wise counsel of his family and friends, then the chances are that my words will fall on deaf ears.

I see a good man as a man of action; a man who spends his life wishing it away, or mourning the chances and opportunities he didn't take, is draining. However, a good man spends time doing the things that he envisions for himself and his family.

Being with a man with such a beautiful mindset creates a sense of safety for me because I know he'd have my back just as much as I'd have his. Our relationship would be inclusive of others, and we'd spend our lives loving each other and those around us.

With all that being said, I will share these words of wisdom with you as you define a good man or woman. First off, as you make your laundry list, be sure you don't allow your superficial requirements to make you miss out on the good characteristics of a potential mate.

Appearances may be important, but in the end, your relationship will only count on how that person acts and treats you. There is always a difference between "Appearance" and "Reality". What if the person you meet has everything you want in a mate, but he has brown eyes, while you require a man with eyes that are blue? Would that fact alone really disqualify him if he were to meet the rest of your requirements? Would having a guy with blue eyes matter *the most* in the relationship? If you were to marry a supermodel-like man with abusive tendency, would his looks matter as much? Would having a man with the physique of a body builder be that important if you end up with a man that is self-centered?

If the girl of your dream were to meet the "baby-got-back" requirement, but she's $1M in debt (and counting), would her voluptuous body matter that much to you? Wouldn't a woman who loves you and has an 850 credit score be better suited for you? These are real things calling for sober reflection as you look at "The List".

I can imagine someone saying, "Sylvia, why can't I have it all?" Well, I'm not saying you can't. All I'm saying is make sure your choices are based on things that matter the most – characteristics that will ultimately make or break the relationship.

The other things I want you to think about are expectations or assumptions we take into relationships. When I was a young adult, I had lots of expectations about how I would raise my children. I saw parents with little kids screaming and falling out in stores. I looked at them with disdain and said, "My child will never act out in public" and "I will never yell at my kids". I had so many wonderful ideas about parenting. In fact, I often say that I did all of my best parenting *before* I had children. Because the truth is, my kids *did* act out in public and I yelled at them too. I, like many other loving parents, lost my cool. My assumptions and my reality didn't quite line up to the way I imagined.

The same is true about dating and marital relationships. We have to manage our expectations about how our mates will respond, what we expect from them, and what we will or won't do. The truth is YOU DON'T KNOW what will happen until it happens. When you approach a relationship with pre-conceived notions based on your fantasies, you are only setting yourself up for disappointment, and your mate may come to feel they aren't good enough for you. I've been there before, and I know how it feels. It's not a good experience.

CHAPTER 5

CAN YOU BE A CHRISTIAN AND BE SEXY?

"That moment – when you walk into a room and light up my world!"

– Sylvia L. Daniels

When we say someone is a good man or woman, we can't ignore the fact that being attractive is part of what appeals to us, more specifically, being sexy. But, the words "Christian" and "sexy" seem to be opposites of each other. Some Christians shy away from using the term "sexy" because it has some negative connotations attached to it. I asked a few of my friends if a Christian man or woman can be sexy. Here's what they all had to say.

Alex is a father of three, and below are his thoughts:

> Me: *Can a Christian woman be sexy?*
>
> Alex: *Yeah!*
>
> Me: *What is sexy?*
>
> Alex: *"Sexy" is a look, an attitude and an overall way you carry yourself. An attitude that is classy and not trashy (that's sexy). Its subtle confidence that radiates in the way she walks and the things she says.*

I asked my friend Janette, a single lady in her late 40s, what her thoughts were about being Christian and sexy.

> Me: *Hey Janette! Can a Christian man be sexy?*
>
> Janette: *Yes! They are the sexiest to me. To see a real man worship the Lord is a really good deal – that's the real deal. When he worships the Lord, to me that's real power. To see it is power in action. To see men crying out to the Father is powerful and amazing. Sexiness is not a tight shirt. I don't like men that just want to be seen – to me that's not "sexy." Neither is a man who is spoiled – that's just Yuck! Ooooo that gets on my nerves!*

Rhonda had another perspective about being Christian and sexy.

> *Yes! A Christian man can be sexy by being respectful, masculine and attractive. His looks and his mannerisms show how smart he is. If he's a gentleman, that's very sexy. A godly man is the best man – hands down!*

Lydia had this to say also:

> Me: *Hey girl! In your opinion, can a Christian man be sexy?*
>
> Lydia: *Absolutely! I just love the sexiness of a man. First of all, God has given us the gift of sexuality. If you don't know it, read the Song of Solomon. God gave us that gift, and we are supposed to use it. I love a man that smells good, looks good, dresses nice and has a sense of humor. What makes a man sexy is his mind. I'm attracted to intelligent men who have compassion and warmth, not men who are intelligent and arrogant with it – making others feel inferior.*

I talked to my friend Michelle – a loving educator in her early 50s about her thoughts. Read her comments below:

Absolutely! Look at the book of the Song of Solomon. It is totally about sex appeal. Well not all of it, but a lot of it is. That book is about the person being physically attractive to the other person. I think there is something extremely sexy about a man who is secure about his identity in Christ. They exude confidence – which is also sexy. Someone who is well groomed, has a sense of style, sense of humor and confidence. A man that takes care of his temple physically is sexy. He doesn't necessarily have to be taller than me, but he can't be shorter (I'm 5' 2"). A man like this would make me feel like he is tailor-made just for me. I think men that have these qualities know how to make women feel beautiful and treasured. I'm not saying how I feel about myself comes from someone else, but I want someone who can express that to me because he has that value within himself.

So what are my own thoughts? For me, a Christian man can be sexy, but that's not so much about how he looks. Don't get it twisted, I like handsome men, but physical appearance is just one part of it. Strength, self-confidence, a captivating smile, commanding voice, kind heart and the ability to draw someone in is incredibly sexy. It's all about "presence" for me! Being subtle is sexy, too. I don't like loud, brassy, bulldoggish personalities because then it's all about him.

Bible-thumping, bible bashing brothers are a complete turn off for me. I prefer the attraction of a man who lives the Word, loves God and unmistakably loves people. That's sexiness at its finest! When I see the people in his life admiring his character and work, that is incredibly attractive to me. A man who loves his children, sacrifices for his family and shows consistency is a perfect example of a sexy man. In other words, what turns me on is someone I can look up to, and someone I can respect! That's incredibly sexy to me.

CHAPTER 6

WILL YOU LOVE ME WHEN...?

"In sickness and in health, for richer or for poorer, until death do us part."

– Marriage Vows

We choose our mates for a number of reasons. Our reasons may be as simple as "she is a successful businesswoman" or "he owns a Lexus." Some choose a mate because they are well traveled or are in the right social circles. Another reason may be because they are charismatic, or quite honestly because they think their mate is drop-dead gorgeous. Those reasons feel very real to us - well, at least they do initially.

The problem with choosing a mate based on these superficial feelings, however, is that they really only address short-term situations. What happens if he loses his hair or her business crashes? What happens if he no longer has the connections that first attracted you to him? What would become of you if you lost your job? Would they still be around you? What would happen if you got sick? Would they sacrificially care for you or would you be left alone? What happens when your love doesn't act in a loving way? Would they love you when you have nothing to offer them other than just yourself? More importantly, would you love them if the same were asked of you?

These are very critical questions calling for honest answers as you think about marrying someone because the consequences of a wrong choice are damning.

A woman I know learned this awful lesson the hard way. She married a man that swept her off her feet. He was charming and handsome, at least in her view. He said all of the right things and made her feel special. After a short time together, she introduced him to her children, and they moved in together. It didn't take long before he began to require lots of her attention. It didn't bother her so much because it made her feel wanted. She catered to his needs and felt she was trying to be the woman he needed in his life. They eventually got married and his neediness grew. She put more time and attention into their relationship and all other relationships suffered, including her relationship with her children.

As time went on, she became ill. Her health deteriorated quickly, and she needed a lot of help. She couldn't wash clothes, cook dinner, clean the house or take care of him in the ways he was accustomed to. She also couldn't take care of her personal hygiene, feed herself or take her medication without assistance. She really needed his help. In response to her need for help, he dropped her off at a local emergency room.

After trying hard to reach her for several days without success, her children were later able to locate her in the emergency room. There she was at the hospital weak, delirious, and unable to talk or eat on her own. She had been there for days without family attention, love or care. Her husband had deserted her.

Her health later improved and she was discharged to a nursing home for long-term care. Her husband rarely visited her and gave lots of excuses as to why he was unable to come. On the rare occasions he did visit, the conversations were typically focused on his issues and needs. The entire time she was there, she longed to experience love from the man that swept her off her feet when she was healthy, but she never did. She felt very lonely because her husband didn't show love to her when she needed it the most. Her final days were spent with heart-wrenching regrets.

That story may seem like an awful retelling of some tragic soap opera, but the truth is, it really did happen. The woman in the story was my mother. I saw this scenario play out with my own eyes, but there was nothing I could do to stop the hurt.

I often reflect on her story while dating. Will this man love me in sickness and in health? Will he be there when I get more wrinkles, or can't do things for him again like before? Will he show a negative attitude if my source of income crumbles? Is he the type of man that'll say, "What's mine is mine and what's yours is yours", or will he cover me financially? I can only imagine men may have similar questions. Would she hold the fort for us if I lost my job? What would happen if I didn't own the things we currently enjoy? What would happen if I became sick - would she take care of me or just neglect me? These are salient interview questions to consider as we consider and evaluate our potential mates.

Let's be honest here. Looks will fade. Finances come and go like the stock market. Social statuses ebb and flow, and healthy bodies become sick over time. If your mate's attraction to you, or your attraction to them, is based on the temporary juicy and shiny stuff that fades quickly, then you should seriously consider the long-term implications, potential heartaches, and disappointment that may accompany your decision. The truth is challenges come to test all relationships in some way, but a relationship that is built on real love and good character has a better chance of weathering the storm.

CHAPTER 7

WORK AFTER THE VOWS

Why Do Women Cheat?

"Pay attention to your woman. Never make her feel single, or she will act as such"

– Anonymous

Your work doesn't stop once you're married; there are definitely some challenges you'll encounter in the course of the journey. One of such may be "infidelity." There's typically a lot of discussions about why men cheat. But, what about the women too?

One of my single male friends once asked me this question. Although, I felt there was much more behind the question than meets the eye, here are just a few reasons why I think women cheat. I'd be remiss if I do not state here categorically that, cheating may happen no matter what a partner does to make the relationship a happy one.

I think some women cheat because they want to fulfill an emotional need rather than just "hook-up". The emotional need can come in different forms, and those forms may vary based on the circumstances and the person involved.

Some women may cheat because they're really not the committed type. They prefer to be in multiple relationships because being in a committed relationship with one person just isn't their thing. She's pretty easy to spot because you won't be able to hold her attention. I'll advise you don't waste your time trying to lock her in.

A woman may also cheat because she is being abused, and someone is playing the role of a hero by protecting her from her abuser. Her emotional attachment and desire to be loved is what pulls her into the cheating zone.

Another reason may be that she wants to get revenge on her man for cheating on her. You've seen the scenario play out time and time again in movies, tabloids, and on social media. A woman finds out her man has cheated on her and betrayed her trust. This makes her feel devastated and angry. He apologizes to her for what happened and promises never to do it again. He expects her to give him a hard time, forgive him eventually, and then allow everything to go back to normal. Some men may even act as if they expect her to have selective amnesia and pretend as if nothing ever happened. Well, some women will do that; they will trust their man and give him another shot at making things right. They may even act as if nothing happened before. While some will be unable to ever trust him again and will choose to walk away from the relationship. But be sure there are some who will let the guy know exactly how it feels to be cheated on.

Here's a question for the guys. Why are men surprised when their wives or significant others cheat on them when they actually did it first? *I'll leave that question there for you to think about.* I've seen many men act as if it is a man's privilege to cheat and a woman's responsibility to remain faithful and forgiving. This mindset is completely unbalanced and unrealistic. Fidelity is the responsibility of both parties. It's not a gender-specific assignment.

By the way, you can cheat on someone without having sex outside of the relationship or marriage. How you may ask? Well, I'm glad you did! Continue reading to find the answer.

Emotional cheating

Your spouse is supposed to be your confidant, your helpmate, and your best friend. He or she is the one who shares your life and your bed. If you have children, they help you raise them. They take care of you when you are sick. Basically, your spouse is there for the good and the messy parts of life.

Your work life is quite different though. You derive pleasure in talking about projects or challenges with a buddy at work. Your work buddy is cool, funny and seems to have a better understanding of what you are facing. And then you both always spend "quality" time working on projects in "conducive" and "serene" working environments that seem intimate enough. In your mind, it's all good because it's platonic. Heck! They may even be married. "Nope! There's nothing going on there. We are just cool friends." That's what you'll always say whenever you're confronted. Huh! Believe me, that's how it starts. It's all a trap.

Many of us spend more time at work than we do at home, and the challenges and trials of work are so significant that we need someone to relate to and synergize with. Your spouse, who has always occupied the center-stage in your life and has been there through thick and thin, has second place in your emotional commitment because your work buddy now occupies that space in your heart. And before you know it, you may start having the feeling that your colleague understands you more, and then start imagining that it would be nice to be with them instead of being with your spouse.

Usher's song entitled *"You Make Me Wanna"* is a good example of a man confiding in a female friend about his relationship challenges. He said, *"You make me wanna leave the one I'm with and start a new relationship with you!"* If we choose to make a colleague our go-to person for emotional support, we're opening the door to emotional cheating.

It's important that we take a close look at how we can defend our relationships against sexual and emotional cheating. The Bible talks about not denying each other sexually (husbands and wives) and also admonishes us to dwell with one another according to what we know about the other person. You can find these scriptures in 1 Corinthians 7:3-5 and 1 Peter 3:7. That places the responsibility of knowing our spouses and fulfilling their needs firmly in our laps. We each have to own it! For many women, love is experienced by having her emotional needs met. If her man makes her feel safe, respects her, and lets her know she alone has his heart and body, she will more than likely be fulfilled by his love. Side note to the Guys: You can't offer her your body and withhold your heart. If you do, you shouldn't expect her to feel loved, or expect anything good to come out of the relationship.

For exclusively dating couples, it's important that you treat this time of exclusivity with care. Your intentions for being exclusive should be to see if the relationship has the potential for love and marriage. If you sense that you aren't fulfilled, and your interest is tilting towards someone else, own up to it. In the words of R&B singer Fantasia, "...*go ahead and free yourself.*" It's ok to walk away because you aren't married yet. You did however give your word to be exclusive, so be true to it by allowing them to move on without disrespecting one another by cheating. Why cause more damage than you have to? The person you are dating is someone else's future husband or wife. Don't make it harder for them to move on to their perfect "better half".

Water Your Own Grass: A Cheater's Story

They were young and in love. He was the answer to her prayers. He loved her and her children too. She loved him and his family as well. After a while, they decided to marry and combine their individualities into one big family. In so many ways, it was a version of the Brady Bunch. For a while, they were happy, in love, and prospering as a family. Unfortunately, life brought its issues. The economy changed, and he lost his job, which affected his ability to take care of his new family unit and pay child support for his kids.

Things grew worse, and he became very desperate to bounce back. Through a get-rich scheme, he got caught in an illegal act and was arrested, charged, and found guilty of felonies, for which he served time in prison. Once he was free, he got into the same difficulty that many ex-felons face: he was unable to get a job because of his criminal record.

It was so hard for the wife to bear the burden of being the breadwinner of the family. But like many strong women, she shouldered the responsibility bravely and did everything possible to make sure the family was well cared for. She worked long hours to provide extra income. He, in turn, took care of the home and the kids. He made sure the kids were dressed and well fed, the house was clean and dinner was ready whenever she came home after a long day at work. They made a difficult situation work well, and their family ran like a well-oiled machine.

After some years, he was blessed with a steady job and the entire family – his wife in particular – was happy for him. Within a short period of time, however, things began to change. He no longer had time to spend with his family. In fact, he would spend more time with his friends. Now you might be wondering, "What's wrong with that?" So many things are wrong with it because he would stay out after work EVERY NIGHT until 4am in the morning.

He began to allow his friends to dictate to him what should be happening in his home. They would say things like, "Man, doing dishes is a woman's job" or "Man! Your wife should do all of the cooking and not you." He listened to the advice of his friends, and things he normally had no problem doing for the family before, now became problematic and a challenge for him.

The change in his attitude made his wife feel lonely, unloved and abandoned by the man she supported for so many years. She thought they were working together, but when things improved for him, he abandoned her and their kids. Once again, she had to bear the burden of taking care of the needs of the large family.

She came in contact with a friend from her past. They shared fun times and had a lot of things in common. They began to spend innocent time together again. He made her feel young, beautiful and needed – like a real woman. She was no longer a woman forced to take up the role of a man because he helped her. She was loved, cherished and pursued by a man who loved spending time with her.

It was overwhelming and intoxicating. Before she could realize what was going on, she had already fallen deeply in love with him. She knew she was faced with a decision that could either make or mar her life and that of her family; she could either chose to stay with the man she was married to, for the sake of her children or leave and be with the man who showed her the love she needed. She chose to stay with her husband and walked away from the man she cared for deeply, even though the decision was tough and hurt her heart. Her husband never changed, but she stayed put anyway.

Well, you may want to applaud her for doing the right thing by walking away and applaud her decision you should. But the question here is, "What made her cheat in the first place?" A hypercritical person might say she cheated because she had an unfaithful heart. One might say she should have spent time more with her kids or put more effort into seeking after her husband. What many of us however, fail to deal with is the root cause of why many otherwise faithful men and women cheat. That root cause can often be neglect – neglect of the basic needs in their lives that their partners forgot, or refused to acknowledge over a significant amount of time.

If your need is quality time and your spouse refuses to spend a significant amount of their time with you, it will leave a gaping hole. You might find it hard to accept the fact that the majority of the time they spend working, watching TV, playing with the kids, on the phone, hanging out with friends or whatever else, is what is hindering them from giving you the attention and quality time you need. It may degenerate to the point where you'll start to feel you aren't worth spending time with but, something or *someone* else is.

A religious person might say, "Well, that's not an excuse. He should be praying and seeking God" or "She should be down on her knees fasting and praying during those times." Again, I won't argue with you there. But here's the deal. The Bible clearly says, "Faith without works is dead." You find that in James 2:17 (KJV). You can pray but if you continue to ignore your spouse's needs, your prayers, fasting and seeking God is in vain. Your abandonment also makes them susceptible to temptation. You can read more about this in 1 Corinthians 7:3-5.

Let's be clear. I am not saying there is a valid reason for cheating because it's not. What I am saying is you can't purposely withhold your part in answering the needs of your spouse and somehow not see that you have a part to play in the outcome.

Ladies and gentlemen, the same is true of any area of love that a spouse needs. As a spouse, YOU are the godly answer to their needs. That is why two separate people will become one flesh at the point of marriage – what is needed by one can now be met by the other.

Companionship, love, sexual gratification, a witness to the ups and downs of life, a best friend, a confidant, a prayer partner, a person to dream and build with – all of those and many more, are the blueprint for marriage. We have gotten so far away from the design and yet we cast all of the blame on the person who cheated, while we *refuse* to address the needs blatantly put in front of us.

There is a saying that, "the grass isn't always greener on the other side." That's actually true, but only if you water your own grass! Have you ever lived in a neighborhood where one homeowner on the block takes great care of their lawn? I mean they water, fertilize, weed and almost militantly care for their lawn. Then, there is the next-door neighbor who barely cuts or waters the grass. The grass is filled with weeds and dry patches from the hot, summer sun. Their lawn is a mess!

Study that other neighbor closely and you may notice he or she is envious of the next-door neighbor's lawn. They may act as if the neighbor has an illegal monopoly on a magical lawn fairy or something. The truth is, all they have to do is the same work their neighbor did to get the same results. There were no magic wands or potions involved; just good, old-fashioned time and sweat equity.

Likewise, you must spend quality time with your spouse and actively engage in being intimately aware of each other's needs. Whatever you do, don't treat getting to know them as a one-and-done deal. Be fascinated with wanting to know them like you did when you were dating. Find out what makes her laugh; what makes him feel good; what things make them tick, or ticks them off. The fact is we all change over time. You will be surprised at what you'll learn. Whether you have lived together for 2 years or 30 years, there are still a lot of things you don't yet know.

There may be exciting desires and adventures waiting to be explored by you.

If you consistently water your relationship, it will be beautiful. If you neglect it, it will shrivel up and die. Your choice, your results!

Tug of WAR! Competition in Relationships

"When we seek to complete rather than compete it is so much easier to cheer each other on!"

– Linda K. Burton

Let's start this out by saying that if you have a competitive spirit in your relationship, it's time to get rid of it!

A man should never feel like he has to compete with his wife, and the same is also true of the wife. If one spouse earns more than the other, the concern should be about increasing the household income and not who makes more than the other. If your spouse makes more than you, celebrate it and appreciate it because their gain is your gain. In fact, you should do whatever you can to help your spouse be productive and balanced in their work and home life.

I knew of a man whose wife was brilliant and talented; so much so that she was recruited for a job that made quite a bit of money. They were struggling financially on his income as a musician, and the new job would change the course of their family. But then the man shocked everyone when he said she couldn't take the job because, to him, "If I don't fly, my wife don't fly either." I remember thinking, "What in the hell is wrong with this man?" Sorry dear reader, but that was exactly what I thought. In that simple statement, he revealed that it wasn't because he felt the job would take her away for long periods of time or somehow have a negative impact on their children. His main concern was that she'd do better than he was doing. The sad thing is that he missed a great blessing embodied in his wife.

It's so ironic when Christian men talk about wanting a "Proverbs 31" virtuous woman but completely miss the part in that same Chapter that talks about the virtuous woman as an astute business mogul who her husband can SAFELY trust. They miss the fact that she owns a thriving business, the community speaks well of her, AND her family doesn't have a single need because she provides for them. Her husband is well respected, and her character brings honor to him as well. She is honored so much that her husband and children call her blessed (Proverbs 3:10-30) KJV.

The Bible certainly doesn't support a competitive mindset so we have to be careful not to miss our favor and blessings because of our egos.

The only exception to competing in your marriage is to see who can out-love the other. Since love is patient, kind, not easily angered, is not envious, keeps no record of wrong, is not self-seeking, believes in the good in others, endures all things and never fails (1 Corinthians 13:4) – a love competition is definitely something to win at.

I know a woman who worked while her husband stayed at home to take care of their three children when they were small. When they looked at the cost for childcare and the special needs of their children, it made sense to handle their family in this way.

He handled the needs of the family at home, and she worked her advertising job without major concern for how to manage the family. To show her appreciation for all that he did for their family, she sent him away for vacations to allow him to rejuvenate. They nurtured their relationship by carving time out for date nights on a regular basis. They worked hard to master the art of winning the love game.

Another one of my friends works at home while her husband works in the corporate world. She cares for the children, manages the house and their finances along with other matters of the household, which allows him to succeed at his company. They make time to stay connected, pray together and love one another. Each person, though not perfect, is winning the love competition.

When you focus on your spouse's needs and love them in the way they need it, you both will win. In that regard, "Let the Competition begin!" And I hope each of you wins Love Olympics gold medals!

Where is the Love?

Ever wonder why spouses lose passion for one another? I mean that toe-curling kind of Eros love that made you want to sing songs, write poems, take long walks and make out under the stars.

I know some would say it's normal for couples to lose passion over a period of time, especially after kids come into the picture. The problem is, I've seen this play out with partners who just started dating, and even older couples who don't yet have kids. After a few months of dating or being married, the fire dies down, the smoldering embers grow cold, and all that is now left is this sour, benign sense of being with a person – almost like being roommates - like unflavored Greek yogurt! You don't go out together anymore. You don't dress up for one another anymore. He stops bringing flowers, and she stops wearing sexy lingerie. She stops cooking nice meals, and he stops doing spontaneous things for her. Before you know it, the relationship stops being dynamic and turns into a daily regimen of room temperature blandness.

The danger then starts to come in when someone starts having the feeling that "he or she is not that into me" and either (A) tries to do something to jump-start the passion (best option anyway), (B) lives with the quiet desperation for passion or, (C) seeks someone else. In case you didn't get this, options B and C are the worse, while option A won't work either if the other person doesn't also get involved.

Our responsibility is to be satisfied with the love of our spouse, and the best way to do that is to consistently make it our life-long *career* to rediscover them every day. The person you dated at the beginning of your relationship enjoyed the love and attention you showered on them when you met. It will take those actions and many more to stay engaged – that's why rediscovery is so important.

If you know your spouse likes acts of service and you did little things to lighten the load or brighten their day when you were dating, what makes you think they will expect something different as time goes on? If she liked yellow flowers when you first started dating, why would you stop giving them to her later? If he liked going bowling with you and friends when you first started dating, why act funny when he wants to do the same thing after you're married?

Longevity should not be rewarded with a cold, boring relationship. Spice it up! Wear that red lingerie! Dance for no reason at all! Go out for dinner once in a while and enjoy being in one another's company. Watch a game together and cheer on your favorite team. You may turn off the TV and look into your lover's eyes. Compliment your spouse when they are not around and let those words of praise catch up to them later. These simple things will allow you to see this wonderful person you gave your heart to, and also fan the flames of passion. The fact is that investment not only increases their quality of life and yours but also creates a satisfying relationship! Who doesn't want that?

Reminiscing about Intimate Days

Poetic Musings

I remember the small bench we sat on after a short walk on our first date. Holding hands and walking to my car with a soft kiss on the cheek.

I do remember when we first made love. You were gentle and yet strong. I remember you calling out my name and laying on my back and kissing me. Tired! Satisfied! Happy! I remember the tears coming down my face as I listened to you. That moment expressed newness and oneness.

I long for days like that. Young love days, basking in each other's presence daily.

Days where I'd get messages with love songs and quick notes with expressed feelings. Drop-ins just to kiss me. Flowers because I love flowers and it was Tuesday. Days when I was sick or troubled, and you came over to wherever I was to make sure I was ok because you *needed* to make sure I was ok.

I remember the morning walks on warm summer days. Talks in the park. Random conversations, questions and laughter.

I so miss those days!

They expressed who I am. I felt free to be who I am with you; random, free to love, open, passionate, introspective and loving.

They expressed who you are; compassionate, strong, caring, loving and kind.

Those days expressed permanence, desire and commitment.

They expressed an intimate knowing - a desire to know and be known.

I long for those intimate days!

CHAPTER 8

COMMUNICATION STYLES

"It's not what you say; it's how you say it. Well, maybe both."

— Unknown

Poor communication is a sure-fire way to kill any relationship quickly. It could be an absence of communication, or more importantly, a lack of the *right kind* of communication.

I have a friend who takes after me in her communication style. If something is on her mind, she avoids cryptic, one-sentence responses. She gives a descriptive explanation about what she is feeling. You don't have to guess what's on her mind because she tells you. All of it!

Another friend of mine is just exactly like that. In fact, he is one of the most open communicators I've ever known. He's very attentive to what people do and say. Sometimes, I feel like I don't have to say a word because he seems to get me before I understand what I'm feeling. At first, I wondered why he was like this. I later learned he pastors a small church and it all made sense.

Have you ever had someone close to you who doesn't seem to understand what you think or feel about a particular situation? It's almost like they don't get why you feel what you feel or respond how you do. It's as though you are speaking a Martian dialect: they just don't get you. I'm sure you have. I've been there, and I've done that myself.

All of this got me wondering about a couple of things. Why do so many couples fail in communication? Even further, why get attached to someone who you know doesn't match your communication style? If you know you are a talker and consistent communication is one of the ways you give and receive love, why on Earth would you even think for a moment about getting into a serious relationship with a person that is as quiet as a church mouse? Wouldn't that drive you AND them nuts? The thing is, I've seen these types of communication mash-ups result in ugly outcomes.

I chatted with some friends about the communication topic some time ago. I asked them about the communication styles they needed in order to have a successful relationship. I also asked about the styles that were a turn-off. Here's what they shared.

Paul and his wife Melanie are 46 years old and have been married for over 25 years. Paul pointed out that one of them is Italian and the other is Mexican. He calls their relationship the "loudness factor." He had this to say about their communication styles:

> *My communication style is loud and blunt, as is my wife's. We both can't stand the communication style that tells a person one thing, they don't mean it, and you only find out when something isn't done. We get heated, but we get the issue out there where it can eventually be solved. I think you need the style that is honest and open, even if that means you get temporarily heated, hurt or upset. I would rather know the truth even if it is not what I want to hear.*

Here's what Bert, a divorcé in his late 40s, had to say.

> *My style is more indirect. I probably show more than I say things verbally. I'm a doer. I need the same in*

a relationship. I guess it's good to hear things verbally, but it's better to show it in indirect ways. On the other hand, I would say there isn't a style I can't handle.

I have a laid-back demeanor, and that helps with it, so I can easily waive off stuff that other people might become abrasive about. I'm like, "whatever."

My friend Tisha is one of those I describe as "softness personified." She's a woman of grace in her 50s. She had this to say about communication styles:

Ok, I've had a chance to think about the question. In a romantic relationship, I want someone who is comfortable with revealing their feelings. I don't have to know every detail of their past or intimate thoughts, but if I get a sense that they're uncomfortable doing so, I will withdraw to ease their discomfort. This sometimes enables the problem (of not communicating) even more. So with my personality, I need someone who is secure enough with himself to reveal true feelings. The thing I hate most in communication is sarcasm. Though not overly, I can be sensitive with those closest to me, and when someone tries to make me feel less than or dumb, I shut down.

Ethan is a handsome 19-year-old teenager. Here are his thoughts about communication styles:

> *My style is direct. I'm not blunt, but I'm more direct when I'm upset, or I'm trying to get the point across. I'm not usually loud, but depending on the circumstances, it can determine my volume. I would rather be with someone who is bold, blunt, and real. I don't like it when people beat around the bush. I don't want to decode the conversation. I feel when someone talks to you; we aren't reading a poem with metaphors. I don't like having to decode. Communicating this way shows maturity to me. If you trust me enough to be with you, why not trust me enough to tell me what's really going on?*

Tasha is in her early 40s. She gave the final perspective on communication. Her style is a little different though. Here are her thoughts about communication:

> *My style is speaking to the individual in love and in truth because I would expect the same. I pray and think about what I want to say versus what my flesh would say, so I can be understood. My style is bold in the way God would want me to be, but I am also quiet when He says I need to be.*

Communication styles vary, and as we've seen here, so do the personality types too. It's one of those important love conversations we need to have in order to have healthy relationships.

The Treasure of Open Communication

One of the things we need to be careful about as we communicate is ensuring that the door to our partner's heart stays open. We can easily close the door of communication by tearing the other person down, making assumptions, refusing to hear them truly, or not being willing to humble ourselves and admit our mistakes. If, for example, you bring an issue up with your spouse and assume they have evil intentions, they will become automatically defensive when you talk to them after a while. The way you treat them will make them think you see them as your enemy. But the truth is, they are actually not your enemy. Yes, they may have made a mistake or may have done something that hurts you, but they are not your enemy. We should lead with this mindset when we communicate.

If you've made a mistake, own up to it. Be sincere in your apologies and work to be better in that area. Since we all mess up and need grace and mercy from God when we do, we should be open to giving the same grace and mercy we so gratefully received.

If your spouse attempts to talk to you about something and you continuously disregard it as over-thinking or a trivial issue, they may withdraw their trust from you. Dismissive behaviors are a form of disrespect.

Open communication is a priceless treasure you can't afford to lose in any relationship. It's a gift you can't buy, but one your spouse offers freely. Don't waste it by failing to realize its value.

When Communication Destroys

"Be sure to taste your words before you spit them out"

- Unknown

You must have heard the old saying, "Sticks and stones may break my bones but words will never hurt me." Right? Well, they lied. That saying is a big, fat, bold-faced, blatant lie! Mean words hurt. They can hurt like hell!

Just because we have the ability to talk does not mean we have the right to destroy people with our tongue. No, we aren't "keeping it real" or "100" when we utter mean words to people. If you keep telling your spouse how miserable you are, or that you wish you had chosen someone else instead of them, they will start to believe you after some time. If all they can look forward to is you spewing regrets, blame, disappointments, and bitterness until the end of time, then you shouldn't be surprised if they decide to leave you sitting there in your pool of nastiness.

As regards to how we should treat one another, the Bible gives pretty clear instructions. In Ephesians 5:33 (NLT) it says, *"So again I say, each man must love his wife as he loves himself and the wife must respect her husband."*

Colossians 3:19 (NLT) says, *"Husbands, love your wives and never treat them harshly."* And Proverbs 15:1 (KJV) says, *"A soft answer turneth away wrath: but grievous words stir up anger."* We see in each of these scriptures that loving one another, showing respect and refraining from harsh treatment and hurtful words are behaviors God wants from us when interacting with one another. The sad thing is, some of us have the tongue of a serial killer when we interact with our spouses (or significant others for that matter).

My advice is that you be careful that you don't murder your relationship with your words. And if you do, don't act wounded if "I'm sorry" doesn't restore the joy and happy moments you enjoyed previously. Proverbs 18:21 (AMP) says, *"Death and life are in the power of the tongue and those who love it and indulge it will <u>eat its fruit</u> and bear the consequences of their words."* Choose your words carefully because you will have to eat the fruit of them later.

CHAPTER 9

TOXIC MARRIAGES & DIVORCES

This subject is a hard one for me to write about really. Over the years, I have talked to many people who have dealt with the pain of divorce and the hard situations that caused them. I've heard perspectives that take a casual stance on divorce, those that are at the middle ground, and those that draw a hard line.

As Christians, we are taught that the only biblical ground for divorce is "fornication." If a man puts away his wife for reasons outside of fornication and marries someone else, he is an adulterer, and the person that marries the woman that was divorced by her husband commits adultery as well. The second thing we are taught is that if you do leave your spouse for reasons other than fornication, you should remain unmarried or reconcile. Most recently, I was told that if a person doesn't physically leave the home, you have to stay in the marriage. (See Matthew 19:9 KJV and 1 Corinthians 7:10-14 KJV). I've been struggling with this a lot.

There are several reasons for this, but before I go there, I'll start with this. I don't want to offend anyone or seem rebellious to biblical scriptures; my heart isn't to rebel against God or those in authority. I honestly tread lightly here because of those reasons. With that being said, I think it's important to take a look at divorce from another perspective.

I agree that a person shouldn't be able to divorce their spouse for frivolous reasons. You shouldn't divorce your spouse because he didn't buy roses, he cleans the house the wrong way, or she burns the food. You shouldn't dissolve the marriage because your spouse doesn't match your new lifestyle or you've outgrown them. The idea that you want someone else because your spouse is too old or because they are sick are not good reasons for divorce. These are all superficial reasons. In these cases, we should do all we can to make it work. With guidance and an open heart, the marriage can become healthy and thrive again.

With that being said, I do however think there are other circumstances that ought to be considered as we look for justification for divorce. Here are a few real-life examples for your consideration.

There's a woman I personally know that was abused by her husband of seventeen years. When I say "abused" I mean, she was beaten, thrown down stairs while she was pregnant, thrown into a glass table, and many other unspeakable things. On top of that, he verbally and emotionally abused her as well. He consistently cursed her, tore down her character, and accused her of cheating on him. He refused to allow her to work outside of the home. His abuse didn't stop with her; he also emotionally and physically abused their children.

For years, she stayed in the marriage because she was afraid; she was afraid of what he would do if she attempted to leave and what others would think if they knew. She was afraid that leaving would mean she wasn't a good wife or a good Christian. Since she wasn't allowed to work outside of the home, she didn't have an income to draw from. She felt trapped because she couldn't take care of her large family. She was also afraid of being alone. As a result of these fears, she stayed put, while the abuse continued for her and the children.

At no point in the marriage was counseling an option. In his mind, she was at fault for what was happening, and as her husband, it was his right to discipline her and the children.

At one point, she finally got enough courage to leave. She took the children and moved to another house. After a while, her husband convinced her he was ready to seek help and have a better relationship. Her oldest daughter pleaded with her not to let him come back, but she allowed him to move in anyway. It wasn't too long before he started beating her and the children again. His final act of abuse was an attempt to kill his wife using a hammer. The oldest daughter walked in on him hitting her mother in the head. She heard him saying "It's gonna be alright" with each blow. Her daughter wrestled the hammer from her father's hand and ran away. While he chased after her, her mother was able to get to safety.

I wish she had a happily-ever-after story, but that was not the case. The trauma of what had been done physically and emotionally affected her. Her self-esteem was destroyed. The long-term effects of abuse were devastating for both her and her children.

In another case, a woman I know lived through years of verbal abuse from her husband. He was often an angry man and it was hard for his wife and children to tell when, and what would make him flare up. The guiding principle for the household was, tread lightly because if he wasn't happy everyone was made to feel it. The measuring stick for many conversations was whether or not it would make him mad.

For the most part of the marriage, he let his wife know he had a better life before getting married. He repeated this over and over again for years. Whenever things went wrong in life, he would always blame her. If he lost his job, and she tried to help him find another one, he would be angry. He didn't finish school, so he blamed her. He didn't get good grades when he returned to school, and he blamed her for that as well. If he had a bad day at work, he brought his negative attitude home for her to deal with.

Somehow, every negative thing in his life could be tied back to marrying her. The ironic thing is when things went well, she was rarely acknowledged for her role. No, in those cases, he would rather give the glory to God or attribute it somehow to his relationship with God. She tried praying, fasting, and seeking both Christian and secular counseling. She even tried changing herself to fit the molds he desired. Unfortunately, it didn't matter what she did; it was never enough, and he refused to be happy.

Although they had marital counseling on several occasions over the two decades of their marriage, the results were the same. If the counselor said anything that placed responsibility on him, he would deny it. But if the counselor said she was responsible for an issue, he made his wife feel ashamed and condemned. As you can imagine, the stress of the marriage began to get to her. She started experiencing depression and panic attacks. She felt overwhelmed and without hope for a better life. She sought biblical counseling from her church's counseling ministry, but after the first session, the minister referred her (and her husband) to the Senior Pastor. During that session, her husband spewed out years of accusations and regrets. She sat in silent shame as he denigrated her in front of the Pastor. The Pastor didn't agree with the husband's way of thinking and how he was treating his wife. He advised him to consider the real genesis of his frustrations and gave him an assignment that would help him understand what he should do.

To maintain the balance, the Pastor also talked to her about walking in maturity. Soon after that counseling session, her husband got angry and moved his family from the church. His grounds for leaving the church were because he felt he was being singled out and picked on.

On the rare occasions that she talked to someone about what she was dealing with, she received well-meaning messages about God hating divorce. She was advised to stay in the marriage and work things out. She eventually got tired of the "well-meaning" speeches and stopped talking about it. She eventually separated from her husband and divorced him a year later, and I will tell you that her life has been better ever since. Her children no longer have restless nights, stomach aches or frequent bouts of depression and she no longer has panic attacks. Their lives are better because she did what she had to do.

So let's take a look at the similarities in these situations. Both women tried to save their marriages. Each wife (and their children) dealt with some form of guilt, depression, anxiety and fear as a result of the long-term toxic marriage. In both cases, each wife suffered harmful consequences for staying in the marriages. One almost lost her life while the other almost lost her mind. The psychological and physical damages to the children only aggravated the consequences. When we compare each situation, we see that each husband felt they were within their rights to treat their families the way they did and each refused to take advice or receive correction.

Now if we look at the Biblical justification for divorce, we see in both scenarios that the husbands didn't leave the marriage or have sex outside of the marriage, so there are no real justifications for divorce. If either woman had remarried, they would have been considered wrong for doing so.

With that being said, why then should these women have to stay in the marriage or stay single for the rest of their lives? Would we allow a victim in any other situation to suffer for the actions of their abuser? No. We wouldn't.

My concern with sexual misconduct and abandonment qualifications is that it leaves so many other reasons - valid reasons - out of the realm of consideration for divorce. When this occurs, it leaves the victim with no possibility of building a loving relationship with someone else in the future if they want to be obedient. It's like saying to the victim, "*You are at fault for being abused, and you will suffer for it for the rest of your life.*" If you look at it well, you'll see it's almost like the messages these women heard from their abusive spouses blaming them for what was happening.

I don't know about you, but my heart breaks when I consider what occurred in these two situations and the imprisonment these women faced because of it. To be clear, I feel the exact same way about men who suffer the devastation of an abusive wife. This isn't a gender issue, but rather an abuse issue.

If we look at other types of abuse, child sexual abuse as an example, we wouldn't expect a child to remain in the care of an abusive mother or father, neither would we expect a child to be exempted from living with a caring family member - going into safe foster care, nor would we exempt a child from adoption because of the harmful acts of their parent. Why then is spousal abuse any different?

I leave you with two final thoughts to consider. Let's say your child - your daughter in this example - was married to either of these men. Would you advise her to stay with an abusive husband? Would you say to her, "Although he's beating you and tearing you down, the Bible clearly says you have to deal with him or remain alone for the rest of your life?" If your answer as a loving parent is "NO!" how much more would the Father want His children to be free and whole?

The second thing I ask you to consider is God's design for marriage. Marriage is designed to mirror Christ's love for the Church. If I may ask, when was the last time Christ cussed you out, beat you or berated you? He hasn't. Christ gave Himself for us to the point of death. He loves us more than He loves Himself. The mystery that marriage is supposed to reflect is the incredible self-sacrificing love that He (Christ) has for the one He loves (The Church - meaning you and me). That is exactly the role of a husband and not an angry, capricious and abusive authority figure.

When a man (or woman) abuses their spouse, they are not reflecting the character of God or being an example of Christ's love for the Church.

As I end this segment, all I ask is that we think deeply about toxic marriages and how we advise people about divorce. If we don't, our advice, though well-meaning, may condemn victims to a life of abuse, loneliness and guilt.

CHAPTER 10

LIFE AFTER DIVORCE

Silence Is Healing

"When was the last time silence was your audience?"

– Arlette Lanae Willis

I divorced my ex-husband after years of hearing him say how unhappy he was for being married to me. He constantly complained about how much better his life was before meeting me, and even more about how much better his life would have progressed without me. I heard this for years. For a long time, I tried to achieve great things so he would appreciate me, but it never worked out. No matter what I did, I never attained being the wife he wanted. It was debilitating really. I was in a state of depression and guilt. I felt trapped and condemned to a life sentence with a man who in essence wished he never met me and quite honestly made sure I knew it.

I took time to be quiet and reflective about my life. That time allowed me to evaluate the state of the marriage. It helped me see that there was hope beyond what I was living with. A time came, and I finally said "Enough" to the verbal abuse. I walked away. And I'm so glad I did.

One thing I hadn't noticed was that, for almost a year, I was busy with some type of activity. I spent lots of my time transporting my kids back and forth to school or taking them out elsewhere. I was working full-time. A lot of my time was spent caring for my sick mother. I spent time moving and unpacking. I had quality time to spend with friends. Did I mention I was in school full-time? Yes! I was busy all of the time, and due to that, I had no real quiet time because my mind was always busy with the activities of life.

One day during summer vacation, I sent my kids away to visit my brother for a week. They had fun and relaxed with no stress. They loved it!

While they were away, I cleaned the house and washed the clothes. I did lots of chores and any other "busy" thing I could do. But when everything was done, I was finally quiet. It was in those gaping caverns of quietness that I finally felt what had been masked for so long. I cried. I cried because I felt heart-wrenching loneliness. My usual smiles couldn't cover the hurt within my heart. I finally felt the pain. I felt betrayed. I felt like a complete fool for getting myself into the situation I was in. I felt stupid for staying so long in a hopeless relationship. I felt like I couldn't trust myself to make good decisions because of my previous ones. All of the feelings that I masked with busyness came crashing in like a massive tidal wave. I couldn't hold them back anymore. I finally came face-to-face with my brokenness, and I hated it.

My brother and I talked after the kids returned home and I shared how I felt with him. He said some things that I will never forget. He first told me that the way I was feeling was a good thing because I needed the time to sort out how I really felt. I agree with him. Silence does allows the healing process to begin. It is the healing environment for us to let the matters of the heart finally surface and be dealt with.

Secondly, my brother told me it's in the silence that we learn who we are and what we want. It is in times of silence that we can focus on the right things that really matter in our lives.

As I write this, I am reminded of the Prophet Elijah. He was afraid of the evil Queen Jezebel who had threatened to kill him. He was afraid for his life, and so he ran away. God told him to go to a mountain and wait there for Him. While waiting to hear from God, there was an earthquake, but God wasn't in the earthquake. After that, there was a hurricane that ripped through the mountain and shattered boulders; God wasn't in the hurricane either. Soon after, there was a great fire, yet God wasn't in the blaze of the fire. After all of the noise died down, Elijah heard the still, small voice of God. It was at that time that he received the comfort from God that he was not alone. It was in the silence that he was able to receive the instructions he needed for the next assignments and tasks in his life (1 Kings 19:11-19 (KJV).

Likewise, it is in the stillness that we are able to see our seemingly impossible situation from God's perspective.

My brother said something further in reference to me feeling stupid because of the choices I'd made. He reminded me that Life teaches you lessons that help you grow and become more mature. Those lessons can sometimes be like a burn. Of course, you know a burn hurts when it happens, just as much as it also hurts while it heals. Once it heals, the surface is tougher than the skin that was there previously.

Similarly, we will become stronger once we allow the silence, times of meditation, prayer, and instruction from God to heal us and bring us into a place of maturity.

Don't fight the silence. Go with it. It's like labor pains. Yes, it hurts like hell. Yes, you would probably prefer to detach from your body and leave the parts having the baby on the table. However, the painful labor process produces the prize of a child. It brings forward someone you have waited for. Silence, when dealt with properly, will produce something similar - the birth of a new "you."

Don't fight the silence – Go with It.

Wilt Thou Be Made Whole?

"I love that this morning's sunrise does not define itself by last night's sunset."

– Steve Maraboli

There is a story in the Bible of a man who encountered Jesus and had a life-altering experience. The man's name is never given, but his experience is an example for us all. You see, the man was like many of us. He was crippled for years. For some of us, it is a physical crippling, but for others, it is an emotional or spiritual crippling. The man, like many others that had physical disabilities or diseases, waited by the pool of Bethesda where an angel would come into the pool and trouble the waters at a certain season in the year (no particular day but a season). Whoever was in the pool first would be healed.

This man had been crippled for thirty-eight years. Although he was near the pool and saw the evidence of the angel being in the pool, he was never able to get in fast enough for him to be healed. (Read about it in John 5: 2-8)

Imagine trying year after year to be healed and never receiving it; it would be tormenting and disappointing. I think Proverbs 13:12 (part A) says it best, "Hope deferred makes the heart sick." (KJV)

The day came, and the Lord came to him and asked a simple question, "Wilt thou be made whole?" But instead of giving a simple answer to a simple question, he responded to Jesus with his circumstances and said, "Sir, I have no man, when the water is troubled, to put me into the pool: but while I am coming, another steps down in before me." (John 5:6-7 KJV). Doesn't that sound familiar? Think about it. Don't we respond the same way?

God, in response to our heart's cry, supplies an answer to what we long for. Perhaps, it is a word of encouragement, an open door that leads out of a hard situation, or the peace we need to stay, thrive and grow in what seems to be an impossible circumstance. Instead of seeing the opportunity of freedom in front of us, we decide to give excuses for staying in the situation and mindset because the answer didn't come the way we wanted it to. Rather than replying with a resounding YES, we give excuses.

My pastor, the late Bishop Benjamin Gibert, preached a sermon about this unnamed man in the Bible. The thing he brought out was that, while the man was looking for the sign of the angel troubling the water (the vehicle for healing),

God already provided someone who was greater than the angel. Jesus the Messiah, The Anointed One, The Savior, showed up to completely change his circumstance, but he didn't recognize the advantage in front of him.

Relating it to today's circumstances, perhaps, we are actively seeking a person (like a counselor, a psychologist, a family member, or a friend) to get us to a place of wholeness. We've been through session after session, and yet no amount of talking works. We use medications to help mask the pain and the anxiety we feel about the issues in our lives, but they don't seem to work, and if they ever do, it's only temporary.

Let me make myself clear here. I am NOT saying seeking counseling from healthcare professionals or friends is bad. No, it's not. It is critically important to have good mental health and seeking help is essential. But when the root of the issue is something only God can deal with, people can only serve as a temporary pain reliever. They are not the source of healing. Those are God's issues to deal with, not Band-Aid-sized issues.

As I described earlier in the book, I have dealt with the pain of divorce. I lived in an unhealthy marriage for a long time. Once I decided I had enough of it and separated, I thought the healing process would be quick. I thought I would get over it and move on immediately with the help of those around me. What I didn't realize was although I talked about it with friends, family, and even a great counselor (who happens to be a Christian), the answer to my issue didn't come from any of them. They are like the unnamed people in the Bible who helped the crippled man get close to the side of the pool of Bethesda. My friends and family did what they could to help, but couldn't really help me get my healing.

You may be curious to know what happened with me. Well, I began to focus on my immediate surroundings. I began to realize there were people who were no longer around. I wondered where all of my friends were during my time of need. I was there for my friends night and day, but I couldn't find them when I felt I needed them most. I believed that if I had the help that I felt I needed, I would heal faster. Or, if I only had someone who loved me and would hold me, I could handle the break up more easily. But, all of these "people crutches" were deceptive because none of them could address the underlying heart issues that only God could heal.

But all along, Jesus was there asking if I wanted to be made whole. My flesh, of course, wanted the "microwave" version of wholeness. I wanted Jesus to speak a word and immediately heal me (and He can do that of course). I wanted the Disney version of healing. I wanted someone to wave a magic wand and "Shazaam!" I'd be instantly healed. Don't judge me; you have probably felt that way too. But what He was offering me was something much deeper; He wanted to heal my heart completely and entirely.

God wants to get into the deep, dark areas of our lives where no one else has been. He wants to heal the large earthquake fault lines and tiny hairline fractures. He wants to heal the results of the words we heard as children, and those we hear as adults. God wants to make whole the areas of brokenness that are the result of our own decisions. Jesus doesn't just heal surface issues alone. In the Scriptures, we see many examples of Him declaring healing and wholeness over people because they had faith. You can see a few examples in Mark 5:25 (KJV) when a woman with a hemorrhaging issue is declared whole and in Luke 17:12-19 (KJV) when ten lepers were healed, but only one was made whole.

Deep within, I realize wholeness doesn't mean I will have spiritual amnesia where my memory will be wiped clean of all of my bad experiences. It doesn't mean that I will have a spiritual download that replaces all of those past memories with newer, refreshing or more palatable memories. What it does mean is that I will be able to forget those things that are behind me, reach for the things before me and push hard towards the prize of the high calling in Christ Jesus (Philippians 3: 13-14 KJV). It means that He is remolding me into someone new, mature, and beautiful in His sight. Ecclesiastes 3:11 (Amplified) says, *"He has made everything beautiful in its time."* It also means that I will have a different mindset as I move forward in life – remembering the grace, mercy, faithfulness, and loving kindness extended towards me. To me, wholeness means a surrendered heart that does not want to go back to the way things used to be. I want Jesus to be able to say to me, *"Daughter, your faith has made you whole!"*

As we journey through this process of becoming whole, delivered, and healed, we won't go back to what held us in bondage. I'm not saying it's easy, but we have to desire it more than we desire the thing(s) that keep us from all God has for us.

Vicious Cycles: Healing Begins With You

"When patterns are broken, new worlds emerge."

– Unknown

I discussed toxic relationships and divorce earlier in the book. The focus was on understanding why we should consider a variety of real issues as valid reasons for divorce and remarrying. But this time, I want to focus on the individual. This segment isn't necessarily just for married couples alone - it applies to single people as well.

The two women in the previous scenarios are real women who were abused by their partners. One of them was verbally assaulted, while the other was physically and verbally abused. Let's keep it real: Women aren't the only ones that deal with abuse. There are similar situations where men are assaulted by women, so this isn't a gender issue. It's an abuse issue.

But, why do people allow abuse in the first place? Let's be honest. We all have wondered why anyone would allow a toxic person to exist in their lives. It seems as though everyone else can see the situation except the person who is in it, right? But, what about you? Have you ever wondered why you allowed a toxic person to exist in your life at one point? Have you ever asked yourself, "How did I get here?" There may not be one simple answer. The abuse cycle can sometimes be very subtle.

There is a fable about boiling a frog alive. The story begins with the premise that a frog will immediately jump out if it is suddenly put into boiling water, which it does. However, if the frog is put into tepid water that is heated up slowly, the frog will not realize the danger it is in. It will continue to adjust to the temperature, and soon be cooked to death. The same is true of toxic relationships. Toxicity is presented in doses, and before you know it, the healthy relationship dies.

The first time it happens, it's subtle. The second time, you may find a way of justifying what happened. Let's say, for example, a friend calls you out of your name. You laugh and go along with it because it was all a joke. The second time they do it, you explain it away by saying "No, it's not what it seems. I'm just being overly sensitive." But, the next time, they take name calling to another level and start cursing. Well, since you've heard them call you names before, you'll think it is ok because they're just being themselves. They didn't mean anything by it. When it happens again, you then believe that you somehow deserved it. You are now internalizing the behavior. And just like the frog, they continued to increase the heat slowly; and you justified and accepted it. *The vicious cycle is now in full effect!* You've become the proverbial frog stew!

How do I break the vicious cycle?

The truth is, toxic relationships require agreement to survive. Vicious cycles are broken when we change our mindset and our behaviors. The pattern ends when we take the blinders off, realize that what is happening to us is wrong and that we have the power to change the situation. We have to take our hands out of the fire.

Walking away from abusive/toxic relationships doesn't mean you aren't a loving person or that you aren't a Christian. Walking away and getting help makes you a healthier, stronger person. God wants us to be in health and prosper even as our soul prospers. You can read this scripture in 3 John 1:2.

Getting Help

I want you to realize that you are not alone. You don't have to suffer and bear it in silence. There are so many of us that have dealt with similar situations and are willing to help you escape, get to a place of healing, and live a peaceful life. If you feel talking to a friend or family member about it isn't comfortable, talk to a pastor or professional counselor. They will help you see a way through what you are dealing with.

If you or someone you know is, or has been a victim of domestic abuse or sexual assault, there are people who care about you and are available to help. You can start by talking to your local pastor or counseling ministers. You can also call The National Domestic Violence Hotline at 1-800-799-7233 or visit them online via www.thehotline.org

God loves you and desires the best for your life. I love you too and that's why I'm sharing this with you. Be brave. Get up and do something. It's time for a change!

CHAPTER 11

LET'S TALK ABOUT SEX

"Honesty is the highest form of intimacy."

– Anonymous

We can't just get through a book like this without discussing the SEX Questions. Direct discussions about sex are not always a part of the pre-marriage conversation for Christians. It's more like a taboo discussion. But I think this has to be discussed openly and honestly. So let's talk about a few popular questions I've heard through my interviews.

Compatibility and Sexual Health

We always talk about our compatibility. But how do you get to know you are compatible with a person sexually if you are not having sex? How do you vet that out?

A friend of mine and I talked about this some time ago. She's was married previously and was abstinent for a few years. She decided not to have sex outside of marriage and made sure the guys she dated knew it and respected it. Having sex within marriage was something she was really looking forward to. Since she was looking forward to "putting it on him" on her wedding night, she wanted to know that the man she would potentially marry had all of his "parts" intact. As with most things, she handled the sex conversation in a very bold and mature way. Rather than beat around the bush about what she wanted to know, she asked him questions about his sexual health and history directly (and tactfully). She asked him questions like, "How many sex partners have you had?" "Do you have a sexual disorder?" "When was the last time you had sex?" "Would you be willing to be tested for sexually transmitted diseases or infections?" "How often do you see a doctor?"

She, in turn, answered similar questions about her sexual health. Since they had built a relationship based on open communication, they took the "sex conversation" in stride as they did all of their conversations.

I asked my friend Antonio what he would think about being asked these questions. He felt questions like these are only for those couples that have expressed an interest in pursuing marriage with their partners, and the conversation should be approached tactfully and respectfully. I agree with him. The issue is not to cause embarrassment but to learn more about the other person and how your combined experiences and opinions may affect your relationship.

Some people aren't open about talking about their sex life. So, what do you do if they don't want to talk about it? If this happens, it's important to try to understand why. It could be that they are uncomfortable with the discussion, or that they feel you haven't dated long enough to have that kind of intimate conversation. When this happens, discuss a situation that would make the conversation easier for them. Your willingness to schedule the discussion shows respect and allows them to become more comfortable about the discussion.

If you've approached the conversation respectfully and tactfully and your partner still refuses to talk about sexual health, you should consider treating the situation as a red flag – one with fireworks and emergency broadcasting system warnings. Something is wrong honey! Get outta there fast!

Do you like to...?

Like the sexual health questions, it is important to have a good understanding of what your loved one thinks about sexual intimacy. Now, I know some will find this to be taboo, but I think it is best to have candid conversations about sexual expectations once you know you are going down the path of marriage especially if you've been sexually active in the past. I've heard a number of horror stories where the husband or wife liked to have sex a certain way, and the other person felt that it was taboo, or ungodly to engage in that type or style of sex. For example, if a spouse believes that the marriage bed is the only ordained place of holiness and feels that the only place you can be sexually intimate is in the bedroom, they may be completely turned off if their spouse decides the living room is the place it's going down that night.

If one spouse feels oral sex is ok while the other feels it's against God's plan for marriage, there may be disagreement and rejection when the latter doesn't respond. Let's say the husband thinks sex toys can spice up the marriage but the wife starts to grasp her pearls at the very thought, there will be some hesitation about exploring sexual boundaries with one another. If one spouse thinks you have to kneel and pray before "partaking in the sex they are about to receive", and the other doesn't want to think about God watching them having sex, someone is going to be turned off.

I asked Antonio about his perspective on communicating and sexual intimacy. Here's what he had to say:

> *A lot of what we feel is (sexual) compatibility is based on knowing how a person is satisfied and satisfying a spouse can come by open communication. So, when your partner communicates their likes and dislikes, you can become what the person needs in the bedroom – if you are willing. The key is having the desire to please your mate, learning what your mate likes, and doing what pleases them.*

Sexual intimacy is not about choosing one person over the other; it's about both partners seeking to please one another. If sex is only about you, then you may find that your spouse feels neglected and used rather than loved and cherished. Sex will become a routine rather than something they look forward to. Let's be honest here, most people don't like chores or boring routines. Who wants to feel like you have to "assume the position" when your spouse wants to be sexually intimate? No one does. The easiest way to handle this important issue is to have heart-to-heart conversations with one another.

If you feel awkward about initiating the sex conversation, make sure you have it as a topic of discussion during pre-marital counseling and marriage counseling. Honestly, it's better to have the conversation up front during pre-marital counseling than have it later when it becomes a problem.

Pornography

"When someone views pornography, they end up creating an intimate bond with an artificial, fake world and can actually lose the ability to bond with real people."

– Family Share

Yes, porn. Seems innocent, right? When it comes to this topic, we hear things like "I'm just looking." "It doesn't mean anything to me at all." "What's the big deal?" "It's a guy thing." These are common responses for a complicated behavior. But is it really innocent? Does casually looking at pornography have a deeper meaning to the relationship or is it really nothing to be concerned about?

I asked my friend Antonio what his thoughts are about pornography. Antonio is a professional, down-to-earth and open-minded.

Me: *Hey Antonio! I've got a question for you that might be a bit risqué. Do you mind?*

Antonio: *No. What's your question?*

Me: *What do you think about pornography?*

Antonio: *I don't agree with it. I think it's like you spying on two people having sex. The Bible says that when a man marries a woman, the union is sacred. I think, when two people come together sexually, God doesn't look at it. If God deems it as personal and sacred, why would we turn it into something commercial?*

When you watch pornography with your man or woman, you are sending signals that it's ok for them to watch another man or woman having sex. You are also sending the same message that it's ok for them to watch it without you. Since arousal occurs when watching porn, you are sending another message that it's ok for your man or woman to want to have sex with someone else. How would you feel if you found your man or woman pleasuring themselves while looking at porn? Would you feel cheated on? How would you feel if they wanted to act what they saw being done on the screen? Like any other theatrical event, it is acting, but when you don't respond the way the actors falsely portray sex, your man or woman will be disappointed. It's like any other gateway drug: it's a high that they will keep trying to recapture and will lead to other things.

Me: *Do you feel watching porn is just a guy" thing?*

Antonio: *When a man gives the excuse that it's a "guy" thing, they are using a reason to excuse themselves and judge women.*

Me: *What do you mean by that?*

Antonio: *Well when a man says that he is saying men can't restrain themselves. He's suggesting that we have a free pass because we are men. Because we feel women can and do restrain themselves, we feel women don't have a free pass. When we give ourselves a free pass, we don't even try.*

Me: *Do you think a person is justified for leaving a person who watches porn?*

Antonio: *That depends. I think it's important for two people to discuss these things and determine what their views are about pornography. One person may grow up seeing porn all of the time so they think it is ok. The other person may have an entirely different view of porn. If you avoided discussing the issue before you got together, it's not fair to get upset the first time it happens. After the conversation takes place, it then becomes an issue of whether or not the person engaging in pornography will give it up or not and whether or not this is a deal breaker for you. If your man or woman says they are not going to give it up and you continue to stay in the relationship, you really don't have a right to be upset.*

I asked Mia, a millennial in her 20s, what her perspective was on pornography.

Me: *If you were in a relationship with a person and found out they watched porn, how would you feel?*

Mia: *I feel like it would bother me because it would make me question if I was good enough for him. I have never heard an instance where somebody watched porn, got into a relationship and stopped watching porn. I believe that it's hard not to view women in general as sexual objects or to objectify women while watching pornography. Watching porn does something to you, and it causes men to see women as mainly sexual beings. When they see women they don't see a woman; they see breasts, thighs, a butt, and a vagina. They no longer see this woman as a real person.*

There is a TED Talk that discusses how pornography sets an unrealistic expectation about how you have sex when it may not be how it's actually done. Pornography is typically one-sided and usually caters for the man's satisfaction. What I heard is that it sets an unrealistic expectation when it comes to sex. Some men think sex equals intimacy - I don't think porn helps with their views on that. All you see is sex...sex...sex...sex...sex! You don't get to see a mental or emotional connection portrayed in porn films. When a porn addict has a relationship problem, they may feel the way to deal with it is to have sex rather than repair the emotional connection.

Me: *You told me how you feel. What then would you do if you found out your man was watching porn?*

Mia: *I honestly don't know. I guess it would depend on the situation.*

Me: *What do you mean by that?*

Mia: *Well, I would at least tell him how it made me feel. I would want to know if someone is watching porn before we got married because it would come to light eventually. If we are in the initial stages of dating, I don't think that it is in my place to say "stop watching porn." I would express my feelings about it, but it would have to be something he wants to do. That's something he would have to want to do for himself. The situation is kinda tricky because porn can be addictive. I've heard some actual incidents where men of God have an addiction and they are trying their best to fight it. I wouldn't know what to do in that situation. If I feel like if it's coming to the point where you are watching it every day, your computer and phone have viruses picked up from porn sites, or if I felt he was objectifying women and disrespecting me, then I would have to break up with him.*

My friend Christine and her husband have been married for more than 30 years. She is a cutie, a mother, a grandmother and a mentor to many. She has given her perspective on pornography in marriage.

I think that if people don't get help with it, it can easily become a sickness. It's deadly and can be deadly to a marriage for sure - that's even when both people are participating because there is something toxic about it. For one thing, it's not something that is meant to be in a marriage. It brings someone else into the marriage. Even though that person is not physically there with you, they are. When your spouse watches that, it brings temporary satisfaction. But overall, it's detrimental.

When Porn Hit Her Marriage

I had a conversation with a friend about her experience with porn. Her husband of several years watches pornography. When Bianca first became aware of it, she noticed he was being secretive about what he was viewing on his computer. Whenever she walked into the room, he'd quickly close his laptop or switch what he was viewing on his phone.

She also noticed that he stayed up late at night and that he wasn't as interested in being intimate with her. One day he wasn't as quick with his reflexes, and she saw pictures of naked women while he was surfing the internet. She was devastated. It was traumatizing to learn that he desired other women. She began to lose trust in his intentions and often wondered if she was good enough for him.

Bianca began to question if she was ever pretty enough, young enough, dressed sexy enough, and whether or not she fulfilled his sexual desires. She also began to wonder if their sexual experiences were mere imitations of what he was looking at online. She was competing with "the other woman" even though the other woman only existed online.

Trust is key to any relationship. Relationships that have no trust foundation won't weather the storms of everyday life. Women and men desire to have an intimate bond with their significant others and spouses – a bond that can't be broken by another person. Since porn brings another person into the equation of intimacy, the bond can be broken irreparably.

Pornography can become an addiction, and it's important to seek help when it does. If it's happening in a marriage relationship, it's important to seek help together because two people have become one in marriage. What hurts one hurts both. If it's happening in an "exclusive" dating relationship, the question should be asked if the word "exclusive" is the right way to describe it. If trust isn't built at this level, it will be hard to expect anything different in marriage.

The Vegas Rule: What Happens in Your Bedroom Stays in Your Bedroom

"Tell your secrets to the wind but don't blame it for telling the trees."

– Khalil Gibran

When I got married at the age of 19, a dear friend gave me some words of wisdom that I held on to religiously. She said, "Don't tell your girlfriends what you and your husband do sexually. What happens in your bedroom stays in your bedroom!"

When she was married, she shared some secrets with a girlfriend. She told her about the loneliness she felt because her husband emotionally abandoned her, the pain she felt because he was verbally abusive, and the anger she felt because he cheated on her on several occasions. She also told her how good he was in the bedroom during the rare times they had sex. Her girlfriend consoled and counseled her to leave him. She was always there to encourage and pay her a visit to cheer her up. She was a good friend.

She came home one day to find the girlfriend and her husband having sex. To say she was devastated is an understatement. She was furious that someone she confided in betrayed her. She never told me what happened next, but I can imagine it wasn't pretty.

My dear friends, I'm passing on similar advice to you. Be careful about sharing what's going on in your relationship with your friends. In many cases, it's better to seek counsel outside of your family and circle of friends to be sure they don't have an offence against your spouse or significant other. A family counselor is an expert in the field and typically impartial to either side of the issue. The other reason is obvious; your so-called confidante *may* be looking for the opportunity to enjoy the person you are complaining about. Since you gave a descriptive idea of what they might need to do or say to get in good with your woman/man, they know the route to take. *What happens in your bedroom stays in your bedroom!* Good advice indeed!

CHAPTER 12

LOVING AGAIN: THE FEAR AND FREEDOM OF LOVE

"Intimacy requires courage because risk is inescapable."

– Rolly May

When you've had a failed relationship or a failed marriage, it could be hard to move forward in life with someone else. Divorce and break-ups hurt. I heard someone describe it as "tearing". I think it's better described as a double amputation without anesthesia. When you still carry the experiences, hurt and shame you felt from one relationship to another, it can be scary in many ways and hard to overcome.

As I write this, I am in a relationship with an amazing, loving and caring man. He's a good dad, respected brother, uncle, and an upstanding member of his community. Did I mention he adores me? (Big smile). You'd think that I would just soak it all in and be in a happy place right? Well, I am. But at the same time, it scares the living daylights out of me because of my constant "What ifs?"

What do I mean by this? Well, I'll tell you. "What if this isn't real?" Like many, I have lived with people who come into my life because of what I can do for them - tangible and intangible things. You know what I mean, right? They are down, you encourage them, their needs are met, and off they go. Once they've gotten all they wanted, they're gone. I find myself putting up a protective barrier as a shield - just in case.

"What if I'm not good enough?" Have you ever felt this way before? I have. I was once in a relationship where I was told over and over again by my spouse that he thought I was something else and implied how much better he and his family were than mine. I heard this for years, and it hurt. Some encounter the "What if I'm not good enough?" issue because their loved one cheated on them and it left them feeling like they lacked something. Others have felt this because their significant other wouldn't commit to them in a significant way. There are many reasons why this question can arise.

"What if this doesn't last?" This question is tricky because it acknowledges that the relationship is good and that both parties see this as the real deal. You both love each other, and things are fantastic for you both. However, this "What if?" robs you because it reminds you that you are totally open to this person and they can hurt you in ways no one else can. All barriers are down – you can't inoculate yourself – there is no bomb shelter. I've honestly thought, "Man, I'm open! What do I do if this doesn't last?" Have you been there before? Trust me; I know how it feels like because I have.

I'm not sure about you, but there are more "What ifs?" I've dealt with. I decided to ask others what theirs are. Here is what Antonio had to say:

Mine would be "What if she's not being completely honest?" I like to know and understand things, so if I'm with someone that is a secretive person, my analytical brain kicks in. I can sense when there is something that is not being revealed to me. When I realize someone is not being completely honest with me, it can lead to detachment. The other side of the coin is that sometimes you can deal with someone who is challenged with honesty or they are unable to be open at the beginning of the relationship. Sometimes, they need time to get to a place where they'll feel comfortable with sharing what is going on.

I'm a big believer in the passage of the scripture that says, "By their fruits, you will know them." (See Matthew 7:20). As an example, I attended a new school (when I was younger), and the teacher brought me to the front of the class and asked me to introduce myself. I did, and she told me she would start me out with an A in her class. Each day, I would have the opportunity to maintain that A through my work and attendance. If I did well, I would keep the A. We need to deal with people in the same positive way and allow them to show us who they are based on our experiences with them. I believe in giving a person the benefit of the doubt. You give them the opportunity to prove themselves. You will learn whether they have good or bad intentions based on what they do over a period of time. When you're dealing with people, see them for who they are and base your decision on that and not on your past."

I asked Tamika, a sassy 42-year-old, what her *"what ifs"* are, and she said, "What *if I don't have anything more to give?"*

Read her reply below:

> *What I mean by that is, sometimes, people get into a relationship where they give everything that they have and more, but their significant other doesn't give enough of themselves. They hold back out of fear. This can happen when someone hasn't evaluated the issues they've dealt with in the past and brings those issues into a new relationship. They end up sabotaging themselves and the relationship. The new person they are with feels the effects of the past relationship though they've done nothing wrong. Nine times out of ten, they will end up back at square one, unfortunately. In order to heal, they have to take time to process what happened in the previous relationship. It's important to receive healing from God and forgive the other person and yourself before beginning a new relationship.*
>
> *This would be an issue for me. I'm allowing myself space, in order to heal, so that I can learn, grow, forgive and be forgiven. When I enter into something new, I don't want to bring anything old with me".*

"What if I can't love them as much as I've loved someone else?"

I can't imagine how it feels to love someone with all of your heart and lose them to death. I have however observed how people express this particular pain. Someone may wonder if he will ever be able to love another woman again after losing the love and support of his amazing wife. He may feel that another person would pale in comparison, or be scared that he has very little to offer because his deceased wife has his heart. Another might wonder if she has the capacity to love as deeply again after the death of her husband or significant other. With time and courage, the idea of opening themselves up to a new partner will become less frightening but it is a significant "what if" in the meantime.

The "*what ifs*" can be scary, but we must be brave, open-hearted and willing to face them in order to experience real love. Love requires risk, but I'm willing to take the jump. Are you?

CHAPTER 13

MY PERSONAL REFLECTION: WHAT DO I WANT OUT OF MARRIAGE? - REAL TALK

I want my best friend! I want a man to be here with me —
here in the physical sense and here in the spiritual sense.
JUST HERE!

I want to experience the mystery of the love between a man
and a woman - a husband and a wife.

I want to know what that kind of love feels like from a
spiritual place. I've heard people talk about it, but I need to
have an experience of it for myself.

I want to know what agreement in a marriage really looks
like. I need to look straight in my partner's face while we
both discuss our dreams, plans and goals in life together.

I no longer want to live an inhibited, pent-up life based on religious mindsets about marriage. I want a God-given love that builds and endures. That's what I really want!

CHAPTER 14

MY FUTURE: HE OFFERED ME MORE

An original writing by Sylvia L. Daniels

"God's heart for me is what's best for me. God's best for me is enough for me."

– Sylvia L. Daniels

Today...

He offered me more than just a ring and his name.

He offered me his eyes.

Eyes that may notice beauty in other woman but will only seek diligently after me.

He offered me his heart.

A heart that remains open to me.

A heart that seeks after God's desire for us.

He offered me his hands.

Hands that are strong. Hands that will do the work of a husband; hands that will cover me; hands that will never rise to cause harm; hands he will raise to give God praise, wipe away tears, fold in prayer, do the dishes, stroke my breasts, caress my face, and block any weapon of harm; hands that will fight for me; hands that will love me.

Today, he offered me more than just a ring and his name.

He offered me his mind – intellectual and quick – engaging and complex – ever growing and therefore always enticing me to seek to know more and explore him more.

He offered me his arms; arms that hold me in the good and the bad times; arms that I will proudly hold as we walk together.

Strong arms I'll admire as he makes love to me; arms of strength as he does his work; arms he'll use to teach children, play sports with friends, or do repairs in our home.

Today, he offered me more than just a ring and his name.

Today he offered me EVERYTHING!

CHAPTER 15

LEARNED TO BE

Poetic Musings

I was strong!

You told me it was better to be timid and meek.

I learned to cower to make you comfortable.

I was smart!

You told me it's better to hide my intelligence because it's
unattractive in a woman.

I learned how to silence my mind and my tongue.

I was joyous!

You told me not to laugh so loudly or smile so brightly. You'll bring attention to yourself.

I learned to be somber.

I was kind!

You told me to stop being so open and acting naively in a cruel world. "Besides, no one will believe you are genuine anyway."

I learned to be suspicious and guarded.

I was ambitious!

You told me it was wrong to seek personal success. Only self-serving people want to succeed. Good people put their ambitions aside.

I learned to be a doormat.

But then I learned you were afraid of my intelligence, my strength, my joy, my kindness and my drive. Like brilliant light, it outshined the darkness and shadows of your fears, your failure and your insecurity.

I learned to be me again. To be fully me and by doing so, I'll change the path of what others Learn To Be.

EPILOGUE

"The people in my life are my life."

– The Landmark Forum

I bet you thought this was the end. But, it can't be. Can it? This book is a journey, not a destination; a journey full of mountains and valleys and opportunities to reflect, learn and grow. While conducting my research for this book, I received many requests to discuss additional topics, but I didn't have time to cover them all in this, one book. It was very hard to contain my writing because there were a lot of important things I wanted to share with you. Needless to say, there will be a "Love Conversations II" in the future. You may choose to call this the first book in the series if you like. But until then, I'll leave you with this final thought for consideration.

The people in my life are my life!

I learned this while attending the Landmark Forum a few years ago, courtesy of a dear friend. I learned this during an important period in my life and I will never forget it.

The people in my life are my life!

The quality of our lives depends largely on whether or not our relationships are poor or great. If you consider all of the things we deem important, in the end, what will matter the most will be two things: our relationship with God (eternal), and our relationships with others. What we will leave echoing throughout time will be the results of our relationships.

With that being said, I hope you invest valuable time in pursuing love conversations with honesty, compassion and genuine interest in what others have to say.

I was blessed to have had so many willing people share their stories and experiences with me while writing this book. Their perspectives are invaluable! I hope you've found them meaningful, and that they've made you think deeply about your current and future relationships. I also hope our experiences touched your heart and inspired you to take a deeper look at how you engage with the people you love.

"Love Conversations" is designed to motivate you to take a good look in the mirror and discover what you really want and need. I hope it pushes you to be honest about what you desire and to be brave about going after it. Most of all, I hope it inspires you to LIVE the best life God truly intends for you!

The people in your life are your life. Make it the best life you can!

Thank you for joining me on this journey.

LOVE CONVERSATIONS: DISCUSSION QUESTIONS

The following questions are for individual reflections, couple discussions, starting a book club discussion or for discussions within small groups. The purpose is to get you talking about the issues in "Love Conversations" and help you continue your personal journey towards healthy relationships.

1.   What is your perspective on the purpose of dating? Is it ok to date for fun?

2.   What do you think is the appropriate time to ask/or be asked "Will you marry me?"

3.   What will you do if you discover that your significant other doesn't desire to marry or pursue

the things you want in life (ministry, children, travel, business, etc.)?

4.   List pros and cons of taking the time to build a relationship with someone you're dating. Have you experienced hurrying in a relationship? What was the most important thing you learned from the experience?

5.   In the section, "A Happy Single Life is the Foundation for a Good Married Life", the author shared Della's story about being divorced, wanting to be remarried but being content while she waited. Use your imagination here: What things might she have learned from being married before? How might what she learned have shaped how she approached singleness, dating and ultimately choosing a mate? How do you think her relationship with God might have impacted her approach to being single?

6.   What passages of the Bible give instructions as to how single people should live their lives?

7.   If you are single, what's on your *To Do List?*" What are you doing to make them happen? As you look at your *To Do List*, how may those experiences shape your relationship with your future mate?

8. What are the benefits of a man pursuing a woman? Are there benefits to a woman pursuing a man? What would you want a person to do when they pursue you? How do love _and_ respect play into the pursuit process?

9. The author talks about confident and dependent personalities. What do you think confident pursuers are looking for in a mate? What characteristics would they shy away from? What are some of the warning signs for spotting dependency in ourselves or in others? What do you think God has to say about having negative dependent behaviors?

10. Do you think it's important to marry someone that is a believer? What behaviors or characteristics would disqualify a person from dating you _even if_ they are a believer?

11. If marriage is your desire, why do you want to get married? What do you think the purpose of marriage is?

12. If marriage is _not_ your desire, why not? How have the things you've seen (or experienced) shaped your viewpoint? Are you open to new possibilities?

13. What is a good man or good woman from your perspective?

14. In your opinion, can a Christian woman or man be sexy? What does that look like from your perspective?

15. The author talks about unhealthy competition in marriages and the importance of focusing on healthy ways to love and support on another. As you look at your current or past relationships, what can you do to show love in ways your spouse or significant other might need them?

16. The author shares her story about her mother's experience with a man that ultimately abandoned her when she became ill. The author also shared how her mother's experience shaped her personal dating choices. Give an example of how your experiences impacted how you've approached dating. Do you think your previous experiences have negatively or positively impacted how you choose or have chosen your significant other or spouse?

17. What is emotional cheating? What is the impact of emotional cheating on your spouse or significant other? What things should you do to guard your relationship against emotional cheating?

18. What is your communication style? What type of style would you like in your long-term romantic relationship? What role does compatible

communication skills play as it relates to how you select or have selected a spouse or significant other?

19. The author admits she struggles with the Biblical grounds for divorce and remarrying. She gave examples where two women left and divorced their husbands for physical and verbal abuse. What are your thoughts about this discussion? How would you advise women or men who are facing abuse in marriage?

20. Do you think it's appropriate to have the "sex talk" with someone *you are interested* in marrying? Is it more appropriate to wait until you are engaged to be married? What are the pros and cons of waiting until you are engaged or married to have the sex talk?

21. How would you start a love conversation about sexual health? What things would you ask and why? What things would you consider to be important or deal breakers as it relates to sex?

22. What are some of the psychological effects of pornography? How might they impact the person watching pornography? How might they impact their spouse? How might it impact a person they are dating? Does pornography reflect God's heart for relationships?

23. The author described how "What ifs?" affect how she and others think about new relationships. How can unresolved "What ifs?" impact good relationships? How have your "What ifs?" impacted the outcome of your relationships? What have you learned from the experience?

24. The author ended with the thought, "The people in your life *are* your life." Think deeply about that statement. Reflect on the quality of your relationships and how they shape your life. What love conversations do you need to have to improve the quality of your life?

ABOUT THE AUTHOR

Sylvia L. Daniels is a native Detroiter. She is an award-winning supply chain diversity professional who has met and dealt with a variety of people and has learned a lot from life and relationships. She is intrigued by the perspectives of men and women - young and old. She believes everyone has a story to tell in life. She is an Author who believes *the people in her life are her life.* She is committed to seeing people have affective love conversations that result in fulfilling relationships. She hopes sharing her ideas and the perspectives of others will help to birth a new story in the love circle so everyone's love story can end with their personal version of "happily ever after."

"Love Conversations: Christian Perspectives about Love and Relationships" is her first book, and it reflects her passion for building relationships that can stand the test of time and weather the storm in all of Life's situations.

REFERENCES

Biblical References

Unless otherwise indicated, all Scripture references are taken from the Amplified (AMP), Christian Standard Bible (CSB), King James (KJV), Message Bible (MSG) or New Living Translation (NLT) versions of the Holy Bible.

Music Lyric References

Easier – Written by Fred Hammond (2012) Album: God, Love & Romance

Single Ladies – Written by Beyoncé Knowles - Carter, Terius "The Dream" Nash, Thaddis "Kuk" Harrell and Christopher "Tricky" Stewart (2008) – Album: I am Sasha Fierce by Beyoncé Knowles – Carter

Free Yourself – Written by Missy Elliot and Craig X. Brockman (2005) – Album: Free Yourself by Fantasia Barrino

Wrecking Ball – Written by Eric Church and Casey Beathard (2014) – Album: The Outsiders by Eric Church

In Da Club – Written by 50 Cent, Mike Elizondo and Dr. Dre (2003) Album: Get Rich or Die Tryin'

Pause – Written by Armando C. Perez, Adrian Santalla, Abdesamad Ben Abdelouahid, Ari Kalimi and Urales Vargas (2011) Album: Planet Pit by Pitbull

You Make Me Wanna – Written by Usher, Manuel Seal, Jermaine Dupri (1993) Album: My Way by Usher

Movie References

Madea Goes to Jail – Written and directed by Tyler Perry (2006) Film

Coming to America – Written by Eddie Murphy, directed by John Landis (1988) Film